# The Leadership Paradox

# Terrence E. Deal
# Kent D. Peterson

# The ❧ Leadership ❧ Paradox

## Balancing Logic and Artistry in Schools

Jossey-Bass Publishers · San Francisco

Substantial discounts on bulk quantities of Jossey-Bass books are available to corporations, professional associations, and other organizations. For details and discount information, contact the special sales department at Jossey-Bass Inc., Publishers. (415) 433-1740; Fax (415) 433-0499.

For sales outside the United States, contact Maxwell Macmillan International Publishing Group, 866 Third Avenue, New York, New York 10022.

Manufactured in the United States of America. Nearly all Jossey-Bass books and jackets are printed on recycled paper containing at least 10 percent postconsumer waste, and many are printed with either soy- or vegetable-based ink, which emits fewer volatile organic compunds during the printing process than petroleum-based ink.

**Library of Congress Cataloging-in-Publication Data**

Deal, Terrence E.
    The leadership paradox : balancing logic and artistry in schools / Terrence E. Deal, Kent D. Peterson. — 1st ed.
        p.    cm. — (The Jossey-Bass education series)
    Includes bibliographical references and index.
    ISBN 1-55542-648-4
    1. School principals—United States.    2. Educational leadership— United States.    3. School environment—United States.    4. School management and organization—United States.    I. Peterson, Kent D. II. Title.    III. Series.
    LB2831.92.D42      1994
    371.2′012′0973—dc20                                                93-48709
                                                                            CIP

Credits are on page 133.

FIRST EDITION
*HB Printing*      10 9 8 7 6 5 4 3 2 1                    *Code 9440*

# The Jossey-Bass Education Series

# Contents

# Preface

There once was a time—in reality or at least in myth—when a principal's job was easier. A relatively homogeneous group of students came to school motivated to learn. Parents supported teachers and made sure that students' homework assignments were done. Deeply committed teachers chose the profession out of a sincere dedication to making a difference. The school building itself was a centerpiece and symbol for the community. Many principals enjoyed a level of moral authority equivalent to that of a parish priest or a local sage. One thinks of the legendary Mr. Chips, whose school and boys were his life. The principal in this period was the inspiration and the symbol for the school, and sometimes for the entire community.[1]

By most contemporary accounts—particularly those coming from today's practicing principals—things have changed. The role has shifted toward administering a highly specialized, extensively regulated, and enormously complex human organization. Many schools now seem forced to be less concerned with developing character and a deep craving for learning than with increasing scores on standardized tests and other formal measures of achievement. In effect, schools now are pressed to resemble more closely the detached assembly-line character of factories. Their chief functions are controlling behavior, standardizing procedures, moving students through the process in large "batches," and sorting them into academic and vocational tracks. Increasingly specialized and closely monitored, teachers are now often insecure about their status and future. Because of this environment, they seek the protection and collective influence of powerful associations and unions.

In many cases, principals view their work as that of a professional manager. The official (or unofficial) job description centers on providing order and efficiency rather than on inspiring people, building collaborative relationships, or playing a symbolic role in the school and community. If one examines depictions of the principal's role by many researchers, managerial imperatives form a large part of the job. Take, for example, several studies that describe how principals spend their time solving managerial problems, dealing with student discipline, responding to central office requests, talking with teachers about schedules and routines, and completing a myriad of reports, federal and state forms, and written requests for information. Principals often move from one routine task to another and are frequently interrupted by unanticipated problems, issues, and crises.[2]

Fictional caricatures of principals in *Teachers*, *The Principal*, or *Ferris Bueller's Day Off* often reinforce these less than positive perceptions. Principals are frequently portrayed as distant and bureaucratic. While often exaggerated, these images incite calls for changes in the principal's role, changes that encourage a more inspiring, exciting, value-based focus on building more collaborative, energetic, and meaningful enterprises.

But new demands for symbolic leadership often overlook the need for managing details and coordinating complex and diverse programs and students. In our view, education may be best served by principals who are *bifocal*, who can combine managerial tasks with symbolic sensitivity and passion, who are simultaneously efficient managers *and* effective leaders. At the very least, principals must have the insight to build a leadership team that fosters a commitment toward both producing results and maintaining faith.

### Shaping the Role: Knowledge and Wisdom

A balanced approach requires both knowledge and wisdom; principals need to know their own values as well as understand what makes a school tick. Knowledge produced by researchers is one force that shapes educational changes of all types, including those directed at the principalship. Such knowledge influences global expectations of what principals should be like and how they should conduct themselves.

Wisdom—what principals learn from experience—plays a far less influential role than knowledge in formal training programs. Yet the understanding produced by experience can provide important direction for school leaders. In a few programs, professional wisdom is emphasized and developed, as at the Harvard Principals' Center and other principals' institutes where sharing lessons from experience has developed into an art.[3] The challenge is to mine the experience base for the lessons and wisdom of how to shape educational practice.

## Background

The work of principals and other school administrators is extremely complex, and the way they conceive of their roles as managers or leaders shapes how they think, act, and feel. Bolman and Deal have studied how principals and managers in both the for-profit and educational sectors think about and respond to job-related situations. Their findings show that one's ability as a *manager* is related to the capacity to see and respond to technical, rational issues. Managers help to create direction, order, and stability in order to improve outcomes. But effectiveness as a *leader* is related to the capacity for understanding and responding to situations in symbolic ways. Leaders infuse an enterprise with passion, purpose, spirit, traditions, and values.[4]

In 1990, we wrote *The Principal's Role in Shaping School Culture* to show how combining theory and experience brings out the symbolic, culture-shaping side of the principal's role. This work showed how principals can effectively encourage and shape values, rituals, ceremonies, stories, and other symbolic forms that make work and learning more connected, value-driven, and meaningful.

But as one begins to engage in symbolic actions, it is very easy to forget that managerial requirements and details are also extremely important. Symbolic unity and commitment do not get the master schedule figured out, supplies delivered to classrooms on time, or balance a school's budget. Such logistical details, as every principal knows, can create formidable problems if not attended to. Although management alone cannot make teachers successful, the absence of workable schedules, quality materials, careful plans, or functioning equipment can erode even the most inspirational school leadership.

### Purpose of the Book

In *The Leadership Paradox,* we draw on both knowledge and wisdom to bring information together with the experiences of principals. Through a mixture of "knowing about" and "knowing how," this book provides some new ways of conceptualizing the work of principals and other school leaders and reinforces skills in merging the managerial and symbolic sides of daily activities.[5]

The primary objective of this book is to help principals and other school leaders to see and integrate both important sides of their enormously challenging work. Rather than putting management and leadership into opposing camps, *The Leadership Paradox* treats them as complementary in the work of principals. Our schools need people who can embrace and blend both the technical and symbolic sides of their role with confidence and enthusiasm, skill and insight.

The book is written to help educators see new leadership and management opportunities in the complicated problems, puzzles, and paradoxes that they face daily. We believe that principals, superintendents, school board members, and other school leaders can actively shape the role that they occupy, rather than be the passive implementors of directives from elsewhere. By harmonizing technical and symbolic aspects of their roles, school leaders can increase their impact on the learning and development of young people—the nation's future.

### Overview of the Contents

Chapter One illustrates the tension between technical and symbolic approaches in a dialogue between a principal and a superintendent. The underlying conflicts in their debate over a school fence reveal the complexities of school leadership roles. Chapter Two expands in more detail the key roles of technical engineers and spiritual artists and the ways these roles are enacted by two very different principals.

Chapter Three shows the problems and paradoxes that principals face. It examines how bifocal principals can combine technical and symbolic approaches to make their daily work more consistent and more influential. Chapter Four provides an in-depth picture of Fran Washington, a bifocal principal who blends technical and symbolic roles in the flow of work. The chapter describes how she uses her position to balance the daily, weekly, and yearly calendars.

Chapter Five shows how schools can blend technical and symbolic aspects of the organization to become more balanced and successful. Chapter Six describes the paradoxes and challenges of improvement efforts and the ways that school leaders can integrate roles to increase the likelihood of successful educational change. In Chapter Seven, we return to the complexities of work and forecast the future challenges of becoming and being a bifocal principal.

*January 1994*                                   Terrence E. Deal
                                                  *Nashville, Tennessee*

                                                  Kent D. Peterson
                                                  *Madison, Wisconsin*

# Acknowledgments

Any book like this draws on a wide range of support and feedback. We have enjoyed these, both from the academic community and from the world of schools. We owe a debt of gratitude to those who have provided ideas and contributed experiences to this effort.

Specifically, we would like to acknowledge the assistance of a number of people who reviewed the manuscript, including two anonymous readers (commissioned by Jossey-Bass), R. Bruce McPherson, Sherrill Wagner, Sharon F. Rallis, and a number of graduate students and colleagues. Discussions with colleagues, advisers, and friends have added much to our knowledge of principals and to the development of the concepts herein. These individuals all furnished good advice; the shortcomings of the work are ours, not theirs. We have also been blessed with exceptionally talented coworkers. Without the continuing help of Homa Aminmadani and Carol Jean Roche, the many drafts, faxes, communications, and rewrites would have been nearly impossible.

Kubulay Gok, Judy Martin, Michael Sokup, Corinne Solsrud, and Frances Wills expended considerable time and energy in tracking down references, providing feedback, and listening to ideas. The members of various classes at Vanderbilt University and the University of Wisconsin–Madison discussed these ideas with us, helped think through connections and concrete examples, and understand the challenges of managing and leading. In particular, Patricia Bower and Linda Martinez at Vanderbilt provided original material that we draw from in several chapters.

We would also like to acknowledge Lee G. Bolman. Although he was not involved directly with this manuscript, his sixteen-year collaboration with Deal undoubtedly shows up throughout. Bolman and Deal are now so intertwined intellectually that they are almost academic Siamese twins. Bolman and Deal's research is cited officially in the beginning of the book, but we owe a debt of gratitude to Lee for his unofficial influence throughout the work.

Although the book was begun several years before the National Center for Educational Leadership was launched, the end product undoubtedly was helped along by the various studies that fell under the center's auspices. For that help, as well as for the indirect contributions of people at the Center on Organization and Restructuring of Schools, we thank the Office of Educational Research and Improvement, through which both centers are funded. We also want to recognize the assistance of Marshall Sashkin. His support and encouragement for our effort, *The Principal's Role in Shaping School Culture*, got us started in the right direction.

Over the past decade we have visited hundreds of schools in the United States and abroad and have had the opportunity to talk to as many principals. Their experiences, insights, and imaginative ways of leading schools have helped us appreciate the skill, hard work, and sensitivity that go into being a school principal. They have freely shared their professional lives with us, from the bittersweet to the inspirational, and have shown us much about schools and their unique inner-workings.

Our editor at Jossey Bass, Lesley Iura, has been a thoughtful adviser throughout, providing assistance during the entire process.

Without help, encouragement, and sufficient time, no book would ever be written. Sandy Deal and Ann Herrold-Peterson contributed all these to our work, and we are grateful for their support and perseverance as this book was completed. Without their backing, the time and energy would not have been available.

T.E.D.<br>K.D.P.

# The Authors

**Terrence E. Deal**'s career has encompassed several different roles: police officer, teacher, principal district office administrator, and professor. He has taught at the Stanford and Harvard Graduate Schools of Education and is now professor of education and human development at Vanderbilt's Peabody College. He lectures and consults internationally with business, health care, educational, religious, and military organizations. He specializes in leadership, organizational theory and behavior, and culture. He is the coauthor of ten books, including *Corporate Cultures* (with Allan A. Kennedy, 1983), an international best-seller. His most recent book is *Becoming a Teacher Leader* (with Lee Bolman), 1993.

**Kent D. Peterson** was the first director of the Vanderbilt Principals' Institute and is the former head of the National Center for Effective Schools Research and Development. He is currently a professor in the Department of Educational Administration at the University of Wisconsin–Madison and a principal investigator for the Center on Organization and Restructuring of Schools. His research has examined the nature of principals' work and the ways school leaders think, act, and shape effective educational settings. Author of numerous studies about principal leadership, he is coauthor of *The Principal's Role in Shaping School Culture* (with Terrence E. Deal, 1990). His work has been used in training programs for school leaders in the United States, Canada, and Europe.

# The Leadership Paradox

# Chapter One

# Introduction:
# A Fence That Divides

"Ah Dios, ¿por qué me mandas esto?"
Dr. Lydia Mareno[1] muttered to herself at the end of another long
day. The hours had been filled with an endless stream of phone
calls, paperwork, food fights, and children who got off at the wrong
bus stop. It was not an especially unusual day. In her first year as
a principal of Guadalupe Elementary, a school in a southwestern
Pueblo, she had already come to realize that days like this were the
rule—not the exception. But this was still not the end. The superintendent, Leo,[1] was also in his first year. He was about to arrive
for a meeting, and the topic of discussion was to be a fence.[2]

To those unfamiliar with schools or the realities of managing them, the fact that two highly trained professionals would
spend time debating the merits of a fence might seem somewhat
peculiar. But anyone who has worked with educational organizations—especially those who have served as principals—knows that
each school day is chock full of such meetings and events. In these,
people argue endlessly about fences, office supplies, cheerleaders,
gum chewing, and other seemingly mundane issues.

In fact, this particular fence had already inspired considerable discussion. The school board had devoted nearly an entire
monthly meeting to trying to agree on whether the barbed wire on
the top of the proposed fence should angle inward or outward. Now

the matter was to receive even more detailed administrative attention from the superintendent and the principal.

Promptly at the appointed time, the superintendent arrived and was escorted by the school secretary into the office of a tired, slightly apprehensive, awaiting principal. After a few perfunctory greetings, the superintendent got right to the point: "I have a serious matter to discuss with you, Lydia. What do you think you are going to do about the fencing in front of the school?"

In some ways, the new principal had knowingly brought the problem upon herself. Her first official act had been to authorize the immediate destruction of a rotting board fence topped with barbed wire that surrounded the school. The eyesore that marked the school's boundaries had lasted for years even though the faculty and others had repeatedly petitioned to have it torn down. Although a new chain-link replacement had been erected around the rear and sides of the school, the question now was what to do in the front. Currently, there was no physical barrier between the school yard and the Pueblo's street. Concerns from citizens had supposedly been voiced to the superintendent about whether children were at risk. The superintendent was there to find out firsthand what was being done to remedy the situation.

The principal was not that concerned about the safety of students. In her mind, the old structure was more of a hazard to children than traffic on the sparsely traveled dirt road in front of the school. She wanted time to construct a beautiful new adobe wall:

> I feel strongly the need to take this opportunity of community pressure to do something that is both wise and practical. We need to get [the] facilities department to construct a fence that is representative—symbolic—of this school as well as of the community. . . . I look into the eyes of these kids every day, knowing that we have got to develop in them a sense of pride and literal love for this school. I think a fence, an adobe-style fence with archways painted in a color that blends with the rest of the village, could symbolically resurrect feelings of pride in both the students and their parents—not to mention this pueblo.

The superintendent quickly countered with a more austere but equally plausible argument: "But a chain-link fence could be installed immediately. And it would look just fine. Besides, your adobe fence would take a bit of time to construct, not to mention the expense. It just isn't realistic."

At this point, the opposing positions solidified, and the antagonists sat almost literally nose to nose. Each quickly and emotionally escalated the argument. The principal invoked her authority to run the school as she saw fit: "No way, Leo! A sterile chain-link fence is not going up in the front of my school. If I have to get out in front of school this summer and lay every brick myself, I will do it. But I will not have your damn metal monstrosity placed as a cold welcome mat at this school."

Rising to his feet, the superintendent exercised his authority with equal relish: "Do I need to make this a directive, Lydia? . . . Because I will, you know."

Without hesitation, the principal reminded the superintendent that she was not without power and resources of her own: "You can do whatever you like, Leo, but I will make your life miserable and not support anything you need help with in the future if you do not back me up on this."

After this impasse, the principal and superintendent silently walked from the office into the school yard. As they began to walk the perimeter of the yard, the principal broke the silence by describing what the adobe fence might look like. As the superintendent turned toward the parking lot to go to his car, he blurted out, "I'll get back to you about your fence."

It is all too easy to interpret this clash as a war of wills between two strong personalities or as a struggle over power and authority. But the disagreement between the superintendent and principal illustrates a more fundamental issue: the age-old tension between two different views of what is most important in organizations, substance or symbols. In this instance, the views were not harmonized to respond to both rational and symbolic concerns. Instead, they became polarized in a conflict over which was to prevail.

The superintendent's position was a logical one. His concern was that the fence serve its functional requirements, be completed on time, and be constructed at the least possible cost. His viewpoint is entirely consistent with sound management principles. No one would argue with the fact that a school yard should be safe, that a project should be completed on time, or that taxpayers' money should be spent wisely.

The principal, however, had constructed her argument on a different premise, one that focused on the meaning of the fence. She was most concerned about what the adobe wall would represent to teachers, children, and residents of a small New Mexico village. To her, it was more important for the wall to imitate the architectural milieu of the village and reinforce the values and traditions of the school. It should be designed and constructed to reflect rooted, shared values and to symbolize the intimate connection between the school and its community. The aesthetic beauty of the wall would be a source of pride for everyone. The fact that it would take more time and cost more money seemed less important. To her, it was the beginning of a deeper transformation of the school—to reembrace its historical foundations and to move ahead into a promising new future. Although Lydia's argument may be harder to defend rationally, it is the kind that frequently prevails at weddings, holidays, or other special occasions when cutting corners or saving time are not priorities.

The conflicting arguments of Lydia and Leo are embedded in competing traditions that are supported by different assumptions. These have produced two distinct and separate bodies of literature. Principals' views of schools as organizations are influenced by which set of assumptions—rational-technical or symbolic—has guided their formal training or seems to make the most sense in the light of personal experience.

### The Technical Side of Schools

Much of the literature on organizations highlights their technical, instrumental, goal-oriented aspects. It is heavily influenced by the belief that organizations are primarily rational entities. Through careful technical analysis, one can figure out the best way to structure roles and tasks in pursuit of clearly defined goals.[3] Max Weber's well-known elements of bureaucracy[4] find modern expression in structural approaches to organizing, managing, and improving organizations.[5] From a rational perspective, schools exist to accomplish explicit and measurable objectives. They take raw materials (students) from the environment (community) and transform them through teaching and learning (the technology) into the products (well-educated and trained people) that the consumer (society) desires. From this perspective, schools should be organized to achieve these specific technical ends as efficiently as possible.[6]

Most writing and research on management in education (and elsewhere) is heavily influenced by structural, managerially focused concepts and assumptions. Principals are taught to emphasize planning, set clear goals, establish measurable objectives, make decisions, evaluate outcomes, allocate rewards, and engage in systematic, planned change. Through rational analysis, careful management, and conformance to well-defined policies and rules, it is assumed that schools can be run smoothly and made better. Explicit solutions could be identified to solve problems and could then be implemented to achieve clear improvement goals.[7]

Guided by such beliefs, many principals favored structured, programmatic approaches to managing schools. The 1960s and 1970s emphasized management by objectives (MBO) and program, planning, budgeting, and evaluating systems (PPBES). In these, the principal's role was akin to an industrial manager's in defining and implementing relatively straightforward, preplanned, packaged policies and procedures. Many thought that structural changes would be welcomed by faculty and other interested stakeholders.

Little or no attention was paid to the values, beliefs, or personal assumptions of those who were to implement these new practices. This is one reason why these early management efforts rarely achieved their goals. Of course, managing is a factor in achieving high-quality schools. Yet administering schools is a much more uncertain undertaking than a technical approach once led us to believe. Many educational tasks are difficult to analyze, model, and assess. Many perplexing problems and paradoxes surface in every school day. Though some activities (purchasing materials, collecting student achievement data, and scheduling staff development) have strong administrative components and need a principal's management attention,[8] there are other important functions that are less certain and more difficult to deal with. These require a different eye. Without equal attention to the symbolic side of schools, little of any real consequence will ever happen.

## The Symbolic Side of Schools

Research on organizations has also produced a perspective quite different from the rational approach. This tradition traces its roots back to another interpretation of Weber and emphasizes the deeper normative and social dynamics of organizations.[9] These ideas have been continued and expanded in the work of many writers who point to the importance of salient beliefs, core values, and shared symbols.[10]

Through this theoretical lens, principals and other leaders act to represent important organizational values. They use symbols to anchor the faith and confidence of others, to communicate purpose, and to build passionate identification with the school. They are spiritual leaders who seek to balance tradition and continuity with beliefs and values that support innovation. Principals who favor a symbolic orientation focus on the creation of a shared sense of meaning and the development of internal cohesion and commitment. A meaningful organization is created through a consistent reference to core symbols and continuous symbolic activity that reinforces key values and beliefs. These take form as rituals, ceremonies, symbolic roles, metaphors, and stories. Leaders and others engage in such activities because, often unconsciously, they want to experience and communicate deeper purposes and forge strong human bonds among everyone in the school community.

School "management," from this view, is shaped and fostered by a culture, a historically woven tapestry of values, beliefs, and symbols that support an ethos of always striving to do better. The primary mission of the principal and other school leaders is to create and reinforce a culture that provides both meaning and movement.

Recently, the literature on management theory and educational change has rediscovered the cultural side of organizations and the leader's symbolic role in improvement and renewal.[11] This view places emphasis on the ways leaders draw on history to develop and

articulate shared values and traditions. Principals anoint and celebrate heroes and heroines, convene and encourage rituals, create and
support the ceremonial communication of values, and work closely
with an informal cast of cultural players in the school.[12] This perspective encourages school principals to worry as much about how
things are perceived by outside constituents and inside members as
they do about designing specific programs and structures.

These two different approaches have reignited an age-old argument over management and leadership: which is better? The continuing debate creates stressful dilemmas and ambiguities for all
collective enterprises. How do we form organizations that are predictable and efficient, yet inspiring and effective? How do we keep
costs down while maintaining high quality? How do we balance
concerns for efficiency and equity with those of ethics and aesthetics?

### Engineers Versus Artists

Most principals, one way or another, create a personal idea of what
their role means and what really matters. In choosing or evolving
an approach to the principalship, people have several alternatives
to consider. Some figure out how to squeak by until retirement;
others generally lean toward one of the two main options just
discussed.

Rationally oriented principals favor a technical, managerial
approach and are very adept at defining goals, creating policies,
allocating responsibility, delegating authority, coordinating diverse
people and activities, and otherwise ensuring that the school is a
safe, orderly, and instructionally focused enterprise. The schools of
these fine "engineers" are tight ships that produce impressive results in teaching basic skills. People—teachers, staff members, and
students—know their job, and they do it. When they are successful,
they receive positive feedback. When they are not, they hear about
it right away. Technically oriented principals are very much like the
superintendent in the preceding dialogue. While some want a basic
no-frills, no-nonsense approach to school management, others find
highly organized ways to develop structures for shared decision
making and collaboration. In a high-performing Florida elementary school, for example, the principal has color-coded memos so

that everyone knows where the information came from and its
priority status.[13]

But there are costs to management, order, efficiency, and an
exclusive emphasis on outcomes or measurable definitions of effectiveness. Beyond the basic guarantees of security and esteem, people
want more from their work and their school, something more meaningful. Students want to have fun with peers and develop other
aspects of their personality. Instructors yearn for the magical
"teachable moments" that may become part of a student's life for-
ever. In the broadest sense, they want to know that they are making
a difference. Parents want to see a little of what they remember
about schools in the past in more contemporary versions; simultaneously, they want assurance that their child's educational preparation will be better than their own. In addition to providing a
well-skilled labor pool, local communities want schools to be a
source of pride and periodic entertainment. Communities also wish
to feel confident that schools are producing the self-awareness and
creativity that will ultimately allow young people to improve upon
the heritage they will eventually receive.

It is around such intangible, expressive, and value-laden matters that the principal as "artist" excels. Artist-principals seek to
define reality, capture and articulate symbols that communicate
deeply held values and beliefs, and engage people in ritual, ceremony, theater, and play. Their primary motivation is to instill a
deep sense of meaning that makes school a place of the heart, as well
as of head and hands. Artistic principals tell stories, talk expressively
about teachers and students, articulate and exemplify values in their
own everyday behavior, create heroes and heroines, and make memos
and meetings fun—even musical.

Symbolic principals encourage schools that are "museums of
virtue" and "communities of spiritually united believers."[14] They
want an organization where people are loyal, committed, and working together toward something larger than themselves. They want
a special place that everyone can believe in and be proud of. In
another top-performing Florida school, not far from the one with
the colored memos, the principal delights in showing visitors her
most prized accomplishment: a picture book featuring every child
in her school.[15]

Lydia Mareno, in the opening dialogue, is motivated by an artistic orientation. To her, everything about a school is symbolic. The wall she was fighting for represented the spirit of the school and its organic connection to the community. She wanted the best for the students in the school. Building a wall in the ancient style of the pueblo was a way to make that statement manifest. The problem is that both she and the school exist in a world where costs, schedules, and results are also important. So are following the rules, balancing the budget, and making sure that students are mastering basic skills. Like the rational, engineering approach to the principalship, the principal-as-artist motif also has its Achilles' heel. The engineer can overmanage schools so that they become rigid and dehumanizing. But too much reliance on an artistic or symbolic approach can result in underachievement and poor production. The best principals, in our view, find ways to combine these ideas in their daily routines and yearly cycles.

### The Paradox Principle

Most principals experience tension around the expressive and technical aspects of their work. It is like a fast-motion balancing act. Or, reminiscent of the conversation between the superintendent and principal, the tension is externalized in a political tug-of-war. By emphasizing one orientation, principals may lose connection with the other.

There is, however, another option: to accept the seemingly contradictory approaches as a paradox to be embraced and creatively addressed, not to see them as an either-or choice to be made. High-performing organizations have both order and meaning, structure and values. They achieve quality at reasonable costs. They accomplish goals while attending to core values and beliefs. They encourage both fundamentals and fun. They embrace the dialectic between expression of values and accomplishment of goals. They encourage both leadership and management, symbolic behavior and technical activity.

From this perspective, schools have to consider what they produce as well as to what values they hold. They have to focus on results and efficiency as well as on faith and meaning. To blend these two approaches is to accept the complicated nature of the work of leading schools. When school principals or leadership teams attend to both administrative imperatives and the desire to shape a meaningful school culture, high-performing organizations are the predictable result.

Part of the process is selecting a leadership team characterized by diversity rather than uniformity. Artistic principals must often nurture the development of managerially inclined staff and assistants to ensure that details are taken care of, that things are done smoothly and correctly. Engineering-oriented principals identify people who can help them infuse a well-running organization with passion and purpose. By becoming artistic engineers or encouraging well-balanced leadership teams, principals can help develop schools that are efficient and goal-directed as well as deeply committed and meaningful.

Schools are complex places with some of the most inherently difficult challenges in the world. Teaching and learning occur in a varied community of children and adults surrounded by concerned parents, graduates, and neighbors. The challenges include problems, puzzles, and seeming contradictions that need to be deciphered, resolved, or accepted. It takes both technical competence and symbolic sensitivity to get the job done with dignity and grace.

# Chapter Two

# The Technician
# and the Artist

Opposites are often viewed as antagonistic positions requiring a win-lose battle to see which will triumph. That was certainly true in the conflict between Leo and Lydia over what type of fence to build. It is also the case in trying to establish whether schools need more management or more leadership.

Some argue that the main problems of schools are unclear goals, loosely coupled roles, remote supervision, unmeasured outcomes, and insufficient coordination. The solution is to find or promote people into the principalship who are technically oriented, equipped with the skills and ability to tighten things up, get the system headed in the right direction, and hold people accountable for measurable results. The underlying belief is that rational analysis, careful planning, sound decisions, and close supervision can solve most of the problems a school faces.[1]

The opposite side of the argument points to a loss of purpose, passion, and meaning in schools. A spiritual vacuum makes it hard for professionals to believe in themselves and even harder for parents and other stakeholders to maintain their faith and confidence in the enterprise. The best way to remedy the situation is to have school leaders who understand the expressive side of the human experience. Such individuals infuse schools with a sense of pride, passion, and purpose. They weave the school-community together through shared symbols, ritual, and ceremony. Through metaphor and stories, they help people articulate a promising future. The underlying belief is that what makes any organization work is an uncommon spirit, a culture that unites everyone together in a common quest.[2]

In the preceding chapter, we got a glimpse of how these two orientations can clash in specific situations. The task at hand now is to show in even more detail how these different ideas manifest themselves in the everyday lives of two different principals, each with a unique style. The first is a portrait of "Charles Clancy," a principal who is a superb manager of a highly effective school. The second is "Mr. Sage," who runs an equally successful school but in a dramatically different, highly symbolic way.[3]

### Portrait of a Technical Engineer

Jules Gordon and Mary Wiley smiled at each other as they peered through the door into Charles Clancy's[4] office and saw him hunched over the computer, his eyes riveted on the luminous screen. Laconda Summers, the school secretary, laughed aloud from behind them. "He'll be here until he gets that schedule right. I remember one year before school started he stayed here all night." All three laughed. Mary spoke in an appreciative tone. "That's probably why I don't worry as much about opening day as my friends at other schools do. It always goes smoothly, just like everything else here at South High."

Charles Clancy is the principal of South High, a school in a midsized city. His school is a tightly organized, well-run system that works well for teachers, students, and parents alike. People know where they are headed and what they are expected to do to reach their destination. Involvement in decision making through a school council and its several committees gives people ample opportunities to influence schoolwide policies and practices.

Maintaining such an effective, efficient school is more than a full-time job. Clancy spends many hours at school. He arrives early to draft memos, deal with routine details, review schedules, and talk with teachers. He stays late to make sure that band concerts, basketball games, and debate tournaments are orderly and well run. Now a seasoned principal with over twelve years of experience, Clancy is well-liked by his staff, parents, and students. His ability to organize things shows on various measures of the school's performance. South High does well on national tests and in athletics (it has been in the state basketball finals four times in the last five years); it has also been successful in gaining and maintaining strong public support. The band and basketball teams, as well as the instructional program, have exceptionally strong financial and community backing. The teachers are some of the best in the city, and the school equipment compares with many of its wealthier rivals. Whenever an opening occurs in either a certificated or classified position, there are many people who apply. Working at South High is seen as a prestige placement.

Life inside South High is clear, organized, and fair. Teachers get materials and textbooks on time and understand what is expected of them instructionally. Expectations for student performance are high, and students know that "slacking off" will not be tolerated. The school's sense of order puts parents at ease. As one staff member said, "We work in one of the best-run schools in the state. We have whatever we need, have ample opportunities to determine school policy, and there are rarely any surprises. It's easy to feel secure and to know we are doing what needs to be done."

Clancy's attention and energy are applied to supervising every aspect of the school. Each morning, before visiting classes, Clancy dictates a detailed memo to teachers and staff informing them of changes in the daily schedule, making them aware of special activities, reminding them of any reports that are due, and recognizing special accomplishments. On Mondays, Clancy's memorandum also lists the milestones, major events, and in-service workshops for the entire week. His memorandum system is similar to that of the Florida principal cited earlier, although the priority scheme is different. Monday's memos are orange; for all other days, the official color is white. This way, people can quickly tell the difference. It also assists them in keeping their own files straight. Confusion is rare and people publicly acknowledge how good it feels not to be kept guessing or thrown off balance all the time.

Instructional supervision is taken seriously at South High,

and both staff and administrator components are held accountable for linking their efforts to instructional objectives. At the beginning of each semester, Clancy develops a schedule of clinical conferences and observations cross-referenced to the master schedule in his office. Days for make-up observations are penciled in, just in case a teacher is sick on the observation day. He also helps to schedule peer observation conferences and personally covers the classes of participating teachers if he needs to. Frequent meetings with department chairs and the heads of support functions ensure that the performance of everyone is closely monitored and people always have ample feedback.

The clinical supervision model of South High follows closely the format of a major well-known text on the subject. Questions, forms, and final write-up have a set organization, much like the French format for a *thème*. Teachers know they will spend roughly forty-five minutes in the preconference and the same amount of time in the postconference. The principal never misses an observation but also never takes extra time. Descriptions of a teacher's classroom performance are accurate and detailed. Particular attention is paid to the criteria defined in the school district "model of teaching," as well as to other important instructional objectives suggested by the teachers. Discussions about observation and assessment of a classroom lesson stick to the point. There are always one or two comments about a teacher's strengths or weaknesses and considerable dialogue about ways to improve. When department chairs are involved in formal evaluation, they follow a similar process.

Most teachers have calibrated their curricula and teaching with the district guidelines, although the site council makes any additions or deletions to tailor South's approach to the specific clientele of the school. Clancy likes to work with both department chairs and the site council to keep up with ideas from current research and practice. Teachers are often pleasantly surprised by his interest and knowledge of their subject matter. Some of the better teachers find Clancy's questions helpful and often provocative. Some of the alternative approaches to colleague supervision and dialogue have come from Clancy or the school curriculum committee. He regularly supports teachers in their requests to attend conferences or bring in outside experts.

Staffing classes and assigning students take an enormous amount of Clancy's time, even though he works closely with the scheduling committee. He tries to ensure the "perfect" class schedule, reworking it until the day before school starts. The master schedule is also crafted painstakingly and reviewed carefully during the summer. Clancy believes that final class placements cannot be made until the day before school begins. Only then will all the information on student requests and needs be available. For example, when a student began private music lessons late in July and requested a change in schedule, Clancy reviewed the master schedule to see if the request for a different strings teacher could be honored. Final changes are often made—on schedule—the day before teachers return. Though the late changes are at times frustrating for teachers, they know that the schedule is designed to serve students' needs. Parents often comment that their children have never had such effective schedules. Everyone appreciates the absence of disruptive changes once the term begins.

Policies on everything from attendance to cheerleader selection are regularly reviewed or rewritten. The school site council, which includes teachers, students, parents, and administrators, oversees the development of and changes in rules and regulations. Anyone can suggest modifications, and people often do. Clancy wants to have a policy in place that will cover every situation. Otherwise, each day would be spent deciding things on a case-by-case basis, a practice that makes it hard to ensure that everyone is treated fairly. When Clancy heard that a student had been seen shopping with a parent following a doctor's appointment in another city, he suggested that the attendance policy be changed to define such behavior as an unexcused absence from school. The attendance committee agreed.

The selection of cheerleaders—a school activity that generates considerable concern and emotion for many parents and students (one need only read the account of the parent who purportedly hired a thug to harm a competitor's daughter to see the potential for trouble)—is also carefully prescribed. Selection criteria, along with processes for appealing decisions, are specifically laid out.

Frequently, these procedures are reworked to take into considera-
tion any possibility for misinterpretation. Clancy encourages
procedures that "leave as little room as possible for interpretation
and require a minimal amount of subjective judgment, only appli-
cation of the rule." Teachers, students, and parents appreciate the
clarity of the rules and the fairness with which infractions are ad-
judicated. One parent noted that she had "never been in a school
with such a well-organized and fair set of policies. Everyone knows
and accepts the rules."

Clancy's analytic skills help South deal effectively and justly
with student discipline problems. All disciplinary matters are covered by policy. When a decision is required, all the facts are gathered. Making exceptions to the rules sets a precedent and therefore
requires careful deliberation. In one incident, the principal, assistant principal, and discipline board spent three days interviewing
students and staff members about what happened before deciding
what to do. But it is not just student personnel decisions that are
dealt with so systematically. Whatever the issues, Clancy always
spends time investigating, gathering information, and collecting
examples that support his position. The site council and various
school committees are equally attentive to information, careful
analysis, and the importance of making decisions that reflect
schoolwide goals.

As one might imagine, the school handbook is long, detailed,
and extensive. Developed by a committee, it covers all aspects of
student and faculty life. School rules and regulations never overstep
the official contract with teachers or intrude on students' constitu-
tional rights. But all other areas are covered; there is little uncer-
tainty about what is expected. As one teacher says, "It's helpful to
know that the handbook covers a lot of territory, will be applied
consistently, and has been developed in conjunction with the site
council. It makes expectations for students and staff very clear. But
we all had a say in what it says."

South High has an efficient and collaborative school improvement process that has been designed and refined over several
years. It begins with the school council review of several student
outcome measures (test scores, grade distributions, absenteeism, and
so forth), followed by a listing of areas where improvement seems

to be in order. These areas are rank-ordered, with staff members suggesting specific strategies and implementation timelines. Following council approval, department or school-level committees actually take on the job of putting the plans into action. This cycle is repeated every spring.

The school budgeting process is also clear, and the school council is involved in allocating resources. Clancy does his home-work on budgeting and regularly investigates procedures used by other schools in and outside the district. He gathers data on budget expenditures to take to the school board in order to request more funds. School allocations are carefully analyzed each year by the site council. There is little room for political maneuvering. Staff members make written requests linked to school goals in order to receive funds for specific programs or departments. Each request needs a rationale, a specific item request, and approval from the department chair. Clancy knows the budget and its five-year history and shares this with the council. The council is hard to convince— unless a well-reasoned case can be presented.

Clancy's assistance in disseminating information has grown considerably with the proliferation of new ideas, programs, and curricular innovations in the last couple of years. Though always helpful in dispersing information on available workshops and sem-inars, more recently he has helped to develop a monthly newsletter for the staff that highlights local and regional workshops as well as articles, videotapes, and books on current topics. He seems a constant source of ideas and knows the names of staff members who are trying out new approaches. He has helped the curriculum com-mittee set up a professional library, a filing system for articles, and a computer list of staff members in the district using particular innovative ideas. Along with a staff member, he also started a Friday Morning Club to talk about current issues in secondary education.

Unlike many other principals, Clancy has worked with the site council from its inception to help delineate very clearly its role and authority. While other schools are embroiled in conflict over who is in charge of what, the council and principal at South High have worked things out. Even procedural steps for resolving con-flicts have been agreed to and spelled out in advance. The head of the school council recently observed, "At first, I didn't think Mr.

Clancy's insistence on being very specific about goals, roles, and relationships was very important. I thought he was being rigid and bureaucratic. Now that we are well ahead of other schools in making shared governance a reality, I appreciate what he asked us to do. We're not experiencing the confusion or having the boundary battles I hear about elsewhere."

Faculty meetings have a written agenda developed collaboratively between the site council president and the principal and distributed ahead of time. Much of the council's time is spent sharing information about current activities in the school, noting progress on school improvement plans, and discussing upcoming workshops and seminars. The responsibility for chairing the meeting is either in the hands of the council president or shared periodically within the membership.

Teacher selection follows a standard format and involves a wide search for the best candidates. Interview questions are specifically outlined in advance; informal interactions with candidates are encouraged and are officially open to everyone; tours of the building are part of a prospective candidate's selection visit. Teachers, staff members, and students participate in the interviews. The discussion of candidates takes place in the site council. They recommend three candidates to Clancy, who makes the final decision. Nothing is left to chance.

Graduation ceremonies are smoothly orchestrated. The event never runs overtime. Although traditional parts of the ceremony are left unchanged, it seems that each year a new touch is added to the ceremony—always with Clancy's approval.

Like most principals, Clancy spends a lot of time with parents. His parent advisory team meets regularly, and he has a parent "hotline" for pressing issues. The school newsletter keeps both students and parents informed. At all the concerts and sporting events, he talks to parents from the diverse populations served by South High. He periodically seeks out parents who seldom come to the school to see if any concerns are not being voiced. Every two years, parent surveys are collected and analyzed.

The facilities of South High are always in excellent repair and spotlessly clean. Clancy usually notices any missing ceiling tiles, cracked windows, or rotting door frames well ahead of the custodian. His careful attention has paid off. South gets a larger share of the district maintenance budget than any other school. His custodial department is exceptionally efficient and well supplied.

The structure of South High School under Clancy's management blends the principal's authority with collaborative decision making. South is a smoothly functioning, predictable school with a solid reputation. There is little deviation from the schedule of classes, activities, and events. It is the classic picture of a well-run organization—a technical engineer's dream. People know who is in charge, what the rules are, what they are responsible for, how they relate to other people, and when they have done well or poorly. Staff members have a say in school policy. Plans for changes are shared with the site council and appropriate committees. All children learn, and on standardized tests as well as on newer performance-based assessments, they perform better than most. Because of its efficiency and focus, the school receives more than its full share of district resources.

### Technical Leadership Roles

Surveying Clancy's portrait, eight important functions within his role are evident.[5] These include (1) planner, (2) resource allocator, (3) coordinator, (4) supervisor, (5) disseminator of information, (6) jurist, (7) gatekeeper, and (8) analyst.

*The principal as planner*—sets long-range goals and short-term objectives, makes sure that everyone has a say in the school and knows where it is headed, works to operationalize and prioritize goals and to develop concrete actions to achieve desired ends, evaluates progress.

Every effective organization engages in some form of planning. The process of developing plans requires several key steps: (1) gathering and analyzing data, (2) setting concrete goals and objectives, (3) developing action plans, (4) assigning responsibilities, and (5) monitoring progress. Through planning, schools involve a variety of people in identifying problem areas and taking corrective action. Both the process and the principal's role in planning vary from school to school.[6]

*The principal as resource allocator*—determines where resources are most needed to maximize progress toward instructional outcomes; ensures that resources are distributed rationally according to plan, not politically to those who wield the most power.

Without adequate resources (people, funds, supplies), it is impossible for anyone to work effectively. The problem is that there are never enough assets to go around. Everyone thinks that his or her piece of the action needs more to get the job done. The process of allocating capital to individual departments or units would be a constant political tug-of-war unless someone or some group with a view of the entire operation made (or were involved in making) the decisions. Principals play a central role in distributing resources to ensure that shared goals, rather than parochial interests, will dominate the process.[7]

*The principal as coordinator*—makes sure that people know what they are supposed to do, how their jobs relate to others, and who is in charge or accountable for results; arranges the appropriate blend of vertical and horizontal linkage, so that diverse efforts mesh as harmoniously as possible.

Specialization allows people to master and execute their responsibilities with precision. Experts are almost always more effective than novices. Experienced teachers, for example, learn instructional and discipline strategies on the job. Even though someone is well trained, craft knowledge is learned mostly through on-the-job experience.

The problem is that specialization leads to myopia and fragmentation unless individual efforts are coordinated in some systematic way. People in organizations depend on one another. One person's job is always linked to someone else's, either sequentially or reciprocally. In addition to planning, organizations coordinate work in several ways: standardization, command, or mutual adjustment.[8] By standardizing procedures, people know exactly what they are supposed to do and what to expect from others. For example, explicit policies and procedures make it possible for a cockpit crew to function with ease—even if strangers are thrown together at the last minute. Coordinating work can also be done through command, giving one person or group authority to tell others what to do. Both of these are vertical approaches.

Work is also coordinated laterally by mutual adjustment. Either in meetings or on the fly, people synchronize their efforts face to face, making it easy for different specialties to function smoothly together. Each coordination strategy has its benefits and costs. Commands are easy to issue but may not always work. Meetings allow people to make adjustments but take a lot of time. Every school either finds its own mix or endures the chaos. Principals spend a good deal of time coordinating or helping teachers and others to find better ways of integrating their work.

*The principal as supervisor*—observes and monitors work to ensure quality and to provide helpful feedback; lets people know how well or poorly they are doing, outlines directions for improvement, and distributes formal sanctions—rewards for superior performance, penalties for poor performance.

Supervision has two main purposes: (1) helping people improve and (2) rewarding them when they do well or providing sanctions when their performance is not up to par. Monitoring what people do entails looking at either their outcomes or their performance. In schools, outcomes are typically measured by how well students do on standardized achievement tests. Recently, other data such as attendance patterns, graduation rates, and criterion-referenced or performance-based tests are being used to track educational results. Performance on the job or in the classroom is monitored through regular observations. Performance is evaluated by comparing observed patterns to preestablished models or criteria. Improvement plans, promotion, dismissal—and sometimes salary—are linked to how well people do their work. In addition, evaluation conferences outline specific recommendations for improvement. Principals spend considerable time in supervising employees, monitoring educational outcomes, or giving people feedback to help them progress. Their supervision takes many forms, depending on the situation.[9]

*The principal as a disseminator of information*—encourages multiple channels for keeping everyone informed of important schoolwide matters: memos, announcements, meetings, and one-on-one conversations; watches over the information network to ensure that the word is getting out to everyone.

For people to work effectively, they need to be kept informed and up to date. Formally, information is passed along through meetings, memos, and announcements. Informally, news is conveyed face to face or through the grapevine. Effective principals constantly seek or provide whatever it takes to keep everyone current. They are either at the hub of the information network or know exactly where to go to find something or get the word out.[10]

*The principal as jurist*—resolves (or develops just and systematic procedures for dealing with) the conflicts that arise in any school; makes sure that interest groups do not abuse their power or bully others.

No human organization is immune to conflict. Conflict between levels or across units can create energy that is used to solve problems, or it results in chaos that undermines productivity. The deciding factor is how conflict is handled. In many schools, disagreements are avoided or smoothed over until they erupt in destructive ways. In successful schools, conflicts are resolved through bargaining, negotiation, or problem solving. As jurists, principals help schools develop systematic procedures for identifying and resolving existing and emerging conflicts. Where possible, disputes are best solved by those involved; if no resolution can be reached, the parties take the issue to a higher level. Ultimately, the principal may have to help the parties work out their differences or make the decision about how the conflict will be resolved.[11]

*The principal as gatekeeper*—makes sure that proper candidates are selected for positions, ensures that the community's interests are well represented in internal patterns and practices, broadcasts the accomplishments to external constituencies, involves community representatives in planning and other important schoolwide decisions.

Every organization has boundaries separating it from its environment. Who comes in, who leaves, and how the organization relates to its external constituencies require careful attention. As gatekeepers, principals monitor the selection of employees and teachers. They make sure that community interests are represented in schoolwide policies and practices. As gatekeepers, principals sometimes buffer professionals against unreasonable influence from parents and local residents. They make sure that appropriate information is shared with the outside world.[12]

*The principal as analyst*—uses systematic, rational logic to diagnose complex symptoms; orders them into solvable problems or intractable ones.

Across the various managerial functions, technically oriented principals identify, define, and solve problems. As analysts they also review student test scores, student placement, the master schedule, and purchases to understand how resources, personnel, or time are being used. They look for potential problem areas, anomalies, and inefficiencies to bring to the attention of school improvement teams or councils. They rely heavily on systematic logic in getting the facts, analyzing the situation, selecting and trying the best solution, and checking to see how it worked.[13]

In none of these functions is the principal the only manager. Particularly in recent times—with faculty empowerment, total quality management, site-based management, and shared decision making—a variety of people are involved. Responsibilities for making decisions, coordinating activities, allocating resources, supervising and evaluating instruction, and conducting other managerial tasks have been allocated to teachers, parents, and others. But ultimately, the principal is accountable for the efficiency and effectiveness of a school. He or she has the ultimate responsibility but shares authority in keeping the school on track and under control. That is the reason why a comprehensive grasp of what the technical engineer's job entails is so very important. Gaps in what the role means or requires spell trouble as each school day or week unfolds.

## Portrait of a Spiritual Artist

"As Mrs. Watson drove up to the school, first buds on the flowers that ringed the school caught her eye. The tiny splashes of color stood out against the white aluminum building and caused her to recall the days last spring when Mr. Sage,[14] the principal, had planted the flowers. She could clearly visualize him in his blue jeans and on his knees, digging and planting and watering, frequently surrounded by students engaged in conversation with him. Mrs. Watson felt fortunate to work with someone as innovative and committed as Mr. Sage."[15]

Mr. Sage, the principal of Carver Elementary School, is a mirror image of Charles Clancy. His administrative approach is

akin to that of Dr. Lydia Moreno, the principal in the opening
dialogue. He understands that schools are symbolic institutions. As
such, their physical appearance can either foster or dampen a shared
sense of pride. Carver's flowers, like Guadalupe's fence, serve as an
attractive focal point—whether people are officially connected with
the school or part of its surrounding community. Sage's vigilance
about the symbolic aspects of Carver is not confined to the exterior
of the school. As people enter the building, they immediately see
what the school stands for. Its spirit is clearly and quickly visible:
"In the entryway lay a large yellow and blue rubber floor mat de-
picting the school's logo—the rearing Carver Stallion with ten rays
of the sun in the background. . . . Hanging from the ceiling were
the Black History posters each class had made."[16]

The unique character of the school also becomes abundantly
clear to prospective teachers or staff members even before they are
hired. The rigorous selection procedures at Carver immediately signal to prospective members that this will not be a routine assign-
ment—if they are lucky enough to get the job. Mrs. Watson, now
a teacher at Carver, recalled her experience:

> She had been somewhat taken aback by all the people
> in the room—the principal, guidance counselor, cur-
> ricular resource teacher and a teacher who was already
> teaching at the grade level for which she was inter-
> viewing. The questions had been different. Word as-
> sociation. Educational terms. Names of educators and
> theories. Questions like, "What was the last lesson you
> taught that really bombed? What was the name of the
> last children's book you read?" There were questions
> about personal experiences and things that were easy
> to talk about and that almost made it seem more like
> a conversation than an interview but that still told a
> lot about the person. She remembered thinking after
> the interview, "Wow, that was a pretty smart thing to
> ask." Still she had been drained! Mr. Sage had once
> told her that he looked for people who were knowl-
> edgeable, opinionated and, above all, committed. He

wasn't really looking for superstars, just people who worked hard.[17]

Carver School is deeply dedicated to a core value that all children can learn. The value is exemplified in the school's motto, a school Where the Kids Shine. Mr. Sage reinforces this important value in many ways.

*He anoints heroes and heroines.* One of the teachers at Carver noted how routinely Mr. Sage passed out praise. A typical afternoon's announcements delivered via the school public address system provided just one of many examples: "Shining student awards were earned today by Michael Smith, Todd Jones, Alicia Harvey, Melissa Praitt and Stephanie Wilson from Mrs. Ardle's room for following directions. Also, shining student awards to Rob, Tim, Susie, and Rachel from Mr. Tom's room for picking up paper in the courtyard. Thanks, kids! Mrs. Barwock's class earned a shining class award from Mrs. Jones for putting their art supplies back quickly and neatly. Way to go, guys."[18]

*He tells stories.* Mr. Sage opens each school year with a story. One year it was the story of "The Little Engine That Could," a reminder of how hard work and positive thinking can pay off. Another year it was the tale "Nail Soup" that launched the school term:

> The story was about a wise villager who offered to feed the townsfolk nail soup, but informed them that anything they contributed to the soup would make it better. The villagers brought their contributions one by one and subsequently had a feast. Mr. Sage had said to them at the conclusion of the story, "So you see, it is what you add that makes all the difference. What will you add to your nail soup this year to help it grow?" Once school started, he read the book to every class and issued a similar challenge to students—What will you add to your nail soup this year?[19]

*He takes advantage of ceremonial occasions.* Hardly any national holiday passes without some form of symbolic identification with Carver School:

Today's turkey lunch was reminiscent of the one several months ago where Mr. Sage had cooked a Thanksgiving turkey for the teachers. He had video- taped the entire preparation and cooking process and encouraged teachers to watch the tape with their stu- dents. He had really gotten involved with the lesson. He had weighed the turkey. Then he showed the kids how to clean it. Then he had explained how to stuff it while stuffing it. Finally, he had cooked it. All the while he had asked the kids questions. "How much do you think it weighs? Estimate it. Do you think it will weigh the same after it's cooked as it did before it was cooked?" He had inserted the temperature thermome- ter. "What do you think the temperature is? Do you think it's done yet?" In between questions he had ex- plained what each part of the turkey was and what function it served. After the turkey was done cooking he served it to the teachers for lunch.[20]

Mr. Sage's deep appreciation for the importance of ceremony extends beyond Thanksgiving or the opening day of school. Before one Christmas vacation, he greeted students as the buses arrived and led them to the cafeteria, where he served all eight hundred hot chocolate. On Valentine's Day, each teacher received a box of ma- nila file folders (a scarce resource) wrapped in a red ribbon.[21]

*He is aware of himself as a symbol.* Mr. Sage was highly visible in regular visits to classrooms.[22] As he mingled with the students, he seemed conscious of his role in exemplifying the values of Carver. His words were part of his daily deeds. An observer's account describes a typical classroom walk-through:

In one room he had participated in a game of "hang- man" and after a few minutes he excitedly called, "OK, I know the answer now!" and then more calmly, "But I'll write it on a piece of paper," which he did, leaving the paper on the teacher's desk as he left the room. . . . In another room, he asked a little girl, "What do you do when you make a mistake? No, let me show you. Watch. Let me show you a little trick. . . ." He helped her for several minutes before a boy walked up to show him a book he was reading. As Mr. Sage looked through the book the boy asked him a question about it. "I don't know, I didn't read the book. Why don't you read it and let me know?" Mr. Sage replied. . . . In still another room the teacher asked the class, "Is this a new song or a review?" Mr. Sage piped in, "Review." When the teacher asked him how he knew, he replied, "I remember—from the barnyard lesson." . . .

In the next room he read aloud from a poster, "We shall overcome," and asked the students, "And what do you want to overcome?" . . .

Later a boy approached him and said, "Mr. Sage, I want to go to the office and see you." Mr. Sage replied, "You practice a book, then come to read to me in the office." . . . In another room, he asked two girls as he helped them dust high, unreachable spots, "If you don't see it, does that make it clean?" . . .

After completing his walk through he returned to his office where a second-grader was waiting for him. He sat on the office floor, the child intently reading a book to him, Mr. Sage listening with equal intensity. After the child finished reading, Mr. Sage talked with him about the book for a few minutes before sending him back to the classroom.[23]

In countless ways, Mr. Sage himself represents and reinforces the cultural commitments of Carver. He is a physical testimony to what the school stands for. He serves as a highly visible role model for everyone in the school. He is a living logo.[24]

*He uses symbols as reminders of important events and values.* Mr. Sage's office speaks as loudly as his person. It is filled with symbols:

As [a visitor] looks around the office, she noted the brightly colored wooden train on a nearby shelf. The

cars had the words "I know I can" painted on them.
On top of the bookcase was a Ball jar filled with nails
of different sizes and types and fastened to a nearby
bulletin board was one huge shiny nail. On the top
shelves of the bookcase were various professional
books and manuals. The bottom shelf was filled with
children's books. On the end table stood a mirror
with the words "Make that change" written across the
top. . . . The words were in reference to the instructional campaign initiated the last nine weeks of every
school year. Last year the campaign had been based
on Michael Jackson's popular song, "The Man in the
Mirror." The idea had been that change begins with
the person who desires to make the change. The mir-
rors were used to remind everyone that when they
looked into them the person they saw was the one
that needed to make the change.[25]

Mr. Sage's influence is an important factor in creating a
school knit together by a tight, organic latticework of values, beliefs, symbols, and ceremonies. At Carver School, it is evident that
teaching is more than just a job, and learning is joyful and fun
rather than drudgery and repetition. Teaching seems almost magic,
and instructors appear to be deeply dedicated to serving the needs
of children and wholeheartedly committed to the school. Sage is a
*spiritual artist* who has infused Carver with meaning, magic, and
purpose. He exemplifies the generic components of symbolic leadership—well within the grasp of any school principal. Stepping
back from the description of Mr. Sage, we can identify the essential
elements of symbolic leadership.

## Symbolic Leadership Roles

Symbolically, the role of principal has eight key aspects. These roles
include (1) historian, (2) anthropological detective, (3) visionary,
(4) symbol, (5) potter, (6) poet, (7) actor, and (8) healer.[26]

 *The principal as historian*—understands the present situation by reconstructing the school's past crises, challenges, and suc-

cesses; hears and recounts stories of past heroines, heroes, and leaders.

A good principal understands his or her school—its historical patterns, the underlying purposes they serve, and how they came to be. Trying to be a leader of something not fully understood is a surefire recipe for stress—and ultimate failure. A principal and other school leaders must inquire below the surface of what is happening to formulate a deeper explanation of *what is really going on*. To be effective, principals must read the deeper culture of their schools and communities.[27]

Reading culture takes several forms: watching, sensing, listening, interpreting, using all five senses, and even employing a sixth or seventh when necessary. The leader must first listen to the echoes of school history in everything that happens. The process of constructing an "organizational genealogy" or family tree is one of the best strategies of coming to know the personality (or culture) of a school. A principal can reconstruct the history through listening to storytellers, watching the drama of school life as it unfolds, interviewing key old-timers, and examining artifacts and records of past successes, crises, and ceremonies.

A more active recreation of school history through group storytelling is both instructive and helpful in connecting a school with its ancestral roots and cultural beginnings.

*The principal as anthropological detective*—listens for and gathers clues to the school's present routines and rituals; assesses existing norms, values, and beliefs; unearths the informal network.

A principal listens to the key voices of the present. These people may be thought of as cultural "players" in various dramas at the school. Experienced principals will recognize immediately the cast of characters and the important informal roles they play.[28] The cast includes:

- *Priests and priestesses*—longtime residents who "minister" to the needs of the school. They hear confessions, preside over rituals and ceremonies, and link the school to the ways of the past.
- *Storytellers*—who recreate the past and personify contemporary exploits through lore and informal history.
- *Gossips*—who keep everyone current on matters of importance,

as well as trivia. They form the informal grapevine that carries information far ahead of formal channels of communication.

* *Spies, counterspies, and moles*—who carry on subterranean negotiations that keep informal checks and balances among various power centers in the school. Through such covert operations, much of the work of the school is transacted.

Each of these sources—with others—informs leaders about the present as well as the past. Far below the level of rational discourse and public conversation, the informal network provides a regular update on the current culture of the school.

*The principal as a visionary*—identifies and communicates hopes and dreams for the future of the school; along with staff members, continually refocuses the purpose and mission of the school.

Just as important, symbolically aware principals listen carefully for the deeper dreams that the school community holds for the future. Every school is a repository of unconscious sentiments, expectations, and hopes that carry the code of the collective dream—the high ground to which they collectively aspire.[29]

These represent an emerging energy that the principal and other school leaders can tap and a deep belief system to which they can appeal when articulating what the school might become. Developing a shared vision for the school that is tied to its most firmly held values and hopes can motivate staff and community alike.[30] Understanding these values makes envisioning a future possible. It helps make a single vision into a collective one.

*The principal as symbol*—affirms values through demeanor, behavior, concerns, attention, and routines. Who a principal is—what he or she does, attends to, or seems to appreciate—is constantly watched by students, teachers, parents, and members of the community. All these communicate what the principal values.

How a principal learns the lay of the land communicates an interest, concern, or disdain for existing traditions, rituals, or larger ceremonies. Once in the position, all that the principal does, says, and reacts to signals the values he or she holds. Above all else, a principal is a teacher in the best sense of the word—teaching through symbolic actions.

Like other managers, principals engage in an enormous number of very routine actions. Taking care of the school building, budget, staff, discipline, and schedule takes time. But these actions can be transformed into more meaningful events that reinforce the basic values and purposes of the school. This reinforcement occurs when routines become rituals, actions imbued with values.

We rarely "see" the symbolic value of an action at the time it takes place. More often, we realize it later, if at all. For example, the building tour that many principals take in the morning may be simply a walk through the building to investigate potential trouble spots or building maintenance problems. But in some schools, teachers and students view the same walk as a ritual demonstrating that the principal cares and is involved in the learning environment, that the principal values their part of the school.

Routine tasks are most likely to take on symbolic meaning when the principal shows sincere personal concern for core values and purposes while performing them. Every classroom visit, building tour, or staff meeting can be an expression of the deeper values the principal holds for the school.

Almost all actions of the principal have symbolic content when a school community understands their connection to shared values and deeper purpose. The community may see a signal in many of the arrangements or behaviors of the principal. These values are communicated in a number of ways.

### The Office

The principal's office, itself a powerful image, communicates a message through its location, accessibility, decoration, and arrangement. These reflect the principal's values. Social artifacts signal to others what is considered important enough for continuous display.

### The Principal's Demeanor

The kind of car the principal drives, his or her clothes, posture, hand gestures, facial expressions, sense of humor, and personal idiosyncrasies send signals of formality or informality, approachability or distance, concern or unconcern. A wink following a reprimand can have as much influence on a child as the verbal reprimand itself. A frown, a smile, a grimace, or a blank stare—each has a potent effect. Their combination means much.

### The Use of Time

How principals spend their time and what they focus their attention on are strong indications about their values. The community quickly discerns discrepancies between espoused values and actual ones by what issues receive time and attention. The appointment book and daily routines demonstrate what a principal really cares about.

### What a Principal Appreciates

Principals signal their appreciation formally through official evaluations as well as public recognition and rewards. Informally, their daily behavior and demeanor communicate their preferences concerning teaching, behavior, and cultural traditions. Teachers and students are particularly attentive to the values displayed and rewarded by the principal in moments of social or organizational crisis within the school.

### The Principal's Writing

The form, emphasis, and volume of memos and newsletters send as strong a signal from the principal as what he or she writes in them. Memos may be a source of inspiration, a celebration of success, or a collection of bureaucratic demands, rules, and regulations. Even the physical appearance of written material will be noticed, from the informality of the blue smudge of the mimeograph to the care evidenced by the new typewriter ribbon or laser printing. Pride, humor, affection, and fatigue are all displayed in writing.

Taken together, all these aspects of the principal's behavior, conscious and unconscious, form a public persona that carries symbolic meaning. Being a symbol comes with the territory of being a principal. His or her symbolic actions help to shape the culture of the school.

*The principal as potter*—shapes and is shaped by school heroes and heroines, rituals, traditions, ceremonies, and symbols.

A principal may try to shape the elements of school culture (its values, ceremonies, and symbols) the way a potter helps clay find its form—carefully, patiently, with much skill and attention to details. A good potter feels the material so it can help guide the shape that the work will ultimately take.[31]

In shaping school culture, a principal articulates the shared values, celebrates school heroes or heroines, observes rituals and ceremonies, and nurtures important school symbols.

### Articulating Shared Values

Shared values often are developed collaboratively. But it often falls to the principal, formally and informally, to articulate the philosophy of what the school stands for. A valuable service is rendered if the principal can express those values in a slogan or symbol that makes them memorable and easily grasped.

### Celebrating School Heroes and Heroines

There are important individuals in most schools, past and present, who exemplify their higher values. Heroes and heroines, living and dead, serve as role models for others. Students, teachers, parents, or custodians—anyone—may qualify for special status.

Examples of local heroes motivate and teach the ways of the culture. When they exemplify qualities a principal wants to reinforce, he or she may recognize these individuals publicly. Schools can commemorate teachers or administrators in pictures, plaques, or special ceremonies just as businesses, hospitals, or military units do.

### Observing Rituals

The school principal can shape a culture by participating in and encouraging the rituals that celebrate important values. Everyday tasks take on added significance when they symbolize values. School activities may become rituals when they express shared values and bind people in a common experience. These rituals are stylized, repeated behavior that reinforce shared values and beliefs.

Rituals take various forms and occur throughout the school year. Some rituals are social, and others center on work. Americans shake hands, Italians hug, and the French kiss both cheeks when greeting or parting. Surgical teams scrub for seven minutes, although germs are destroyed by modern germicides in thirty seconds. British artillery teams, when firing a cannon, still designate one member who holds his hand in a position that once kept the horse from bolting because "that's the way it has always been done."[32]

Meetings, parties, informal lunches, and school openings or closings provide opportunity for rituals. Some schools often end faculty meetings with an opportunity for anyone to share anything of importance. In this setting, issues can be aired, accomplishments recognized, disagreements expressed, or exploits retold. These rituals bind people to each other and to the deeper values of the organization.

### Observing Ceremonies

School ceremonies are occasions to put cultural values on display, to retell important stories, and to recognize the accomplishments of important individuals or groups. These special events tie past, present, and future together into a stronger social fabric. They intensify the social commitment to the organization and revitalize individuals for challenges that lie ahead.

When a ceremony is held, the place, unusual touches, and a special rhythm and flow may build momentum and express sincere emotions. The planning and staging of these events are often done with extreme care. Encouraging and orchestrating special ceremonies provides another opportunity for principals to shape—and be shaped by—by the culture of the school.

The observation of national and seasonal holidays, from Halloween to Presidents' Day, may make the school an important cultural center for events in the local community and reaffirm ties to the wider culture. Such festivals provide an opportunity for students to learn a variety customs and foods. They create a schoolwide unity around differences that could otherwise become divisive.

*The principal as poet*—uses language to reinforce values, communicate educational beliefs, and support cultural norms; sustains motivation and focus through clear, consistent messages.

We should not forget the straightforward and subtle ways that principals communicate with language, even in informal conversation. The words and images and feeling principals use to talk about the school or students convey sentiments as well as ideas. "The achievement scores of my school are above the norm" conveys a very different image from "Our school is a special place to be." Also, as storytellers, principals become the bards of their cultures.[33]

Acronyms can separate insiders from outsiders to the school community. SAT, CTBS, or NAEP may carry different meaning for educators and the public. Idioms and slogans—such as We Care; We Dare; We Share—may condense shared understandings of school values. However, the potential hypocrisy of such slogans is often alienating. Consider the satirical book *Up the Down Staircase*, in which the principal would say, "Let it be a challenge to you" in the face of problems that were obviously impossible to solve. To be effective, a slogan must be tied to beliefs in an honest and consistent manner.

Metaphors may provide "picture words" that consolidate complex ideas into a single, understandable whole. Whether students and teachers think of a school as a factory or a family will have powerful implications for day-to-day behavior. In one school, the principal speaks of the school as a "sanctuary" for children from difficult homes.

One of the highest forms of principal "talk" is the *story*. A well-chosen story provides a powerful image that addresses a question without compromising its complexity. Stories ground complicated ideas in concrete terms; they give them a flesh-and-blood reality. Stories carry values and connect abstract ideas with emotions and events.

Stories told by or about leaders help followers know what is expected of them. They emphasize what is valued, watched, and rewarded for old-timers and greenhorns alike.

*Sagas*, stories of unique accomplishment, rooted in history and inspiring to the whole school community, can define the core values of a school to its members. They can convey to the outside world an intense sense of the unique that captures imagination, engenders loyalty, and secures resources and support from outsiders who themselves are seized by the spirit of the place.

*The principal as actor*—improvises key roles in the ongoing human dramas, comedies, and tragedies of the school; shifts roles to reinforce cultural values.

Cultures are often characterized as theater, the stage on which important events are acted out. If all the world's a stage, then aspects of the life of a school are fascinating soap operas, dramas, comedies, and sometimes tragedies. Technically, they have been called social dramas.[34]

Much of this drama occurs during routine activities. Periodic ceremonies, staged and carefully orchestrated, provide intensified, yet predictable, theater. The outcome is usually known in advance (a graduation exercise or a pep assembly), but both the players and the spectators are caught up in the spirit of the play.

There are also moments of unpredictable drama in any organization. Crises or critical incidents (like a student suicide or the explosion of the space shuttle *Challenger*) are moments of unforeseen school drama. Critical incidents provide the principal a significant opportunity to act in a social drama that can reaffirm or redirect cultural values and beliefs.

Drama provides a heightened opportunity to mark a historical transition and reaffirm cultural ties within the school community. Rather than inhibiting or stifling such dramas, the principal may take hold of them as an opportunity to resolve differences and redirect the school. The occasional comedies and tragedies offer further opportunities to shape the culture.

Social dramas are often *improvisational theater* with powerful possibilities to reaffirm or alter values. In a political sense, such events as faculty or student conflicts are arenas—with referees, rounds, rules, spectators, fighters, and seconds. In the arena, conflicts surface and are decided, rather than lingering and seething because they have been avoided or ignored.

*The principal as healer*—oversees regular transitions, painful losses, and change in the life of the school; heals wounds of past and current conflicts to keep the social fabric whole.

Most school cultures are stable but not static, and changes do occur. The principal can play a key role in acknowledging these transitions, healing whatever stress they create and helping the school adapt to change in terms of its traditions and culture. Changes open wounds—some deep, others only on the surface.[35]

Schools celebrate the natural transitions of the year. Every school year has a beginning and an end. Beginnings are marked by convocations to end the summer and outline the vision and hopes for the coming year. Endings are marked by graduations, which usually unite members in a common celebration of the school culture.[36]

The beginning and end of employment are transitions that a principal may also use to reaffirm school culture and its values. What newcomers must learn about the school is a good definition of what is valued and believed by members of its culture. Retirement marks the end of a career and the loss of a member of the school community. A retirement ceremony reviews and commemorates the contributions of the individual and also the ongoing traditions of the school. Both the retiree and the school need to crystallize what the person has meant and the legacy he or she leaves behind.

Even transfers, reductions in force, terminations, and firings for cause are transitions that can be marked by cultural events. In one Massachusetts elementary school, primary students named hallways after teachers who had been let go in the wake of a taxpayer rebellion that required tremendous cost reductions in nearly every school in the state.

Unpredictable, calamitous events, like the death of a student or teacher or a school closing, will be upsetting to all members of the school community. These transitions require recognition of deep pain, emotional comfort, and communication of hope. Unless transitions are acknowledged in cultural events, loss and grief will accumulate.

The principal as healer recognizes the pain of transitions and arranges events that make change a collective experience. Drawing people together to mourn loss and to renew hope is a significant part of the principal's culture-shaping role.

Clancy and Sage have been featured in this chapter because each is a delightful and decided example of a particular approach to running a school. Although each has strengths, some potential weaknesses are also apparent. Over time, South High's shortage of passion and frolic could cause even the most efficient system to become boring and repetitive. At Carver, one wonders how important details are taken care of or just how productive all the fun and drama really are. The ideal situation would be to create within every principal a balance between the two approaches, changing what often is seen as opposition into a tension-filled, flowing push-and-pull of thought and action. If we began to see the roles not as opposite but as complementary, we could open up some exciting new ways for principals to find new possibilities in complex situations that at first seem to require one approach or the other.

# Chapter Three

# The Bifocal Principal

$M$ost Americans are prone to dualistic thinking, to seeing the opposing parts rather than the unifying essence:

> Although at first view nature's poles present themselves as opposite and mutually antagonistic, on closer inspection we realize that they are complementary; one cannot exist without the other. Without the female, there could be no male, and without the male there could be no female. The lungs both expand and contract continuously. If movement in either direction were to stop, life would cease. Were man to know no sadness, he would never know joy; without the experience of failure, he would know no success; without a knowledge of sickness, he would know no health. The universe and our knowledge of it are therefore constituted of the endless to and fro movement of life from any pole to its complementary opposite.[1]

We often see solutions to problems as choices between extreme alternatives; polarities are seldom perceived as the woof and warp of the same fabric. Puzzling situations are simply problems to be solved with predetermined answers rather than dilemmas that may not have a clear solution.

Those who work in schools sometimes apply this view of opposites in thinking about what they do and searching for solutions to problems they encounter. One is either a manager or a teacher, a leader or a follower, a planner or a doer.

In reality, however, these seeming dualities in principals' work are more often integral parts of a balanced composition. For example, a strike over low salaries can be the beginning of a new set of cultural practices in a school. A principal's veto of a new program selected by the school council can trigger a dialogue that lays the cultural foundation for shared decision making. Each new puzzle can contain both technical challenges and deeper philosophical issues.[2]

Dualistic thinking leads people to view managing and leading as different, as inherently conflicting activities. Many administrators thus think they need to pick one orientation over another, to focus mainly on either technical *or* symbolic aspects of their work—but not both. Principals often find themselves in a predicament of trying to figure out who they want to be like, which way to behave, what to emphasize. Should they emulate the management model exemplified by a Leo or Clancy or pattern themselves after the artistic orientation of a Mareno or Sage? Either choice creates its own dilemmas. As Pirsig states, "Because we're accustomed to it, we don't usually see that there is a third possible logical term equal to yes or no which is capable of expanding our understanding in an unrecognized direction. We don't even have a term for it, so I'll have to use the Japanese Mu. . . . Mu means 'no thing'. . . . It states the context of the question in such a way that a yes or no answer is in error and should not be given. Unmask the question is what it says."[3]

Unmasking the question means confronting the possibility that principals can be both leaders and managers, can create both meaning and order. They can be both supporters of change and defenders of the status quo. Principals can find a balance point between being traditional or innovative, tight or loose, inflexible or creative. Principals can embrace paradoxes and puzzles of their work as the fulcrum for creating new approaches to leadership.

The idea of *Mu,* of finding a "nonanswer" to perplexing questions seems strange to us. It introduces the notion of *paradox,* a seemingly contradictory situation or statement that runs counter to common sense and yet appears to be true.[4] How can a pointillist painter like Seurat produce masterpieces of merged colors and complex form with a multitude of closely spaced dots? How can one mix water and salt so that the resulting solution is unique, with no physical evidence of the crystalline form of salt? How does the Möbius strip seem to have three dimensions, yet one is able to draw a continuous line around it, moving onto both sides, and never pick up the pencil or cross an edge (personal conversation, 1993, with Norman Webb, senior scientist, Wisconsin Center for Education Research, University of Wisconsin—Madison)? How can one see both near and far? In schools, complicated puzzles may only be addressed successfully through blended, bifocal actions, those that are both technical *and* symbolic. These are activities that provide simultaneous opportunities for both management and leadership.

### Paradoxes of the Principalship

The dilemmas that arise in schools every day suggest the need for new ways of thinking about how to combine leading and managing. We need to think of leadership as tied with management into a complex knot. This knot is interwoven with the need to manage people, time, and instruction while at the same time infusing a school with passion, purpose, and meaning.

Paul Houston, superintendent of the Tucson Public Schools, for example, developed his "ten teachings for leading by ambiguity" around the philosophy of contradiction and paradox. He suggests that leadership should exhibit

- Interdependent autonomy
- Flexible integrity
- Confident humility
- Cautioned risk taking
- Bifocal vision
- Wobbly steadiness
- Skeptical belief

- Thin-skinned empathy
- Lowly aloofness
- Childlike maturity[5]

Although these ten teachings may appear as incomprehensible, mixed messages to stubbornly dualistic thinkers, they open new possibilities to receptive school principals. They lead to the Taoist concept of *wu-wei*, the place between doing nothing at all and forcing actions no matter what. As Watts writes, "Wu-wei . . . is what we mean by going with the grain, rolling with the punch, swimming with the current, trimming sails to the wind, taking the tide at its flood, and stooping to conquer."[6] Centering on the balance point allows principals to maintain a middle position between the extremes of too much managerial control and overzealous symbolic commitment.

In Taoist traditions, philosophers use the concepts of Yin and Yang to depict opposites that when combined make a unified whole.[7] One thinks of man and woman, love and hate, war and peace, status quo and innovation—each making the other possible. The Yin-Yang concept represents a seeming duality that in fact expresses an implicit unity. In baseball, without the offensive batter there can be no defensive play. In nature, without the death of the caterpillar there is no butterfly. In schools, there can be no new hiring without retirement or transfer; often new programs cannot be instituted without the discontinuation of old ones; and new forms of staff collaboration cannot take place without the end of isolation. Watts notes, "The art of life is not seen as holding to Yang and banishing Yin, but as keeping the two in balance, because there can't be one without the other."[8]

The same need for balance is true of the oft-cited management-leadership polarity. The concept of paradox in a principal's work stresses the ability to embrace these supposedly opposing poles, to become a technical artist or an artistic technician. By merging different, seemingly conflicting roles, school leaders can bring harmony and balance to the situation and deal with complex puzzles at the same time.

Principals address polarities simultaneously as a way of accomplishing at least two things with a single action—shaping culture while developing a plan, promulgating policy through poetry and stories, using traditions and ceremonies to inform and restructure. Every event or situation presents opportunities for leading while managing, managing while leading. For busy principals, this approach creates a new cache of available time. For schools, this helps address the challenge of getting results while maintaining confidence and faith. Ambiguities can be dealt with in a new way, through embracing paradox and seeking harmony among competing values, ideas, and actions. A recent study of three leaders demonstrates how this idea can work.[9]

## Good Leaders Give Mixed Signals

Several years ago, Bower studied three highly effective leaders to uncover the reasons for their success. Over a three-year period, she observed and interviewed a hospital administrator, a grocery-store manager, and a high school principal. She also interviewed their subordinates. She was particularly concerned with how these leaders send signals to and receive them from subordinates. She found some interesting patterns that illustrated paradoxes in their work and demonstrated how they balanced leading and managing.[10] The three leaders communicated in a variety of ways. They sent signals

- Of what is expected, appreciated, and preferred by "being with" rather than "being around" people
- Through questioning that promotes the belief that subordinates are the experts
- Through the selection and installation of new members
- By nurturing a defined cultural core causing members to remain faithful
- Informally through the network of cultural carriers
- Through open, inclusive, and high-variety communication
- Through a common vocabulary keyed to an ethic of service and a spirit of collaboration
- Through the content and manner of staff development
- By maintaining the facility to highlight values of pride, care, and commitment to quality
- By serving themselves as signals[11]

These patterns are consistent with those found in the contemporary literature about leadership and management. They are also consistent with many of the ideas we have already presented about the various ways in which principals deal with their organizations. But as she probed more deeply into her interpretation of the behavior of these three leaders, she made some unexpected findings. Given prevailing assumptions about effective leadership, she had expected that the leaders would give clear, consistent signals. Instead, she found their signals were seemingly mixed and contradictory yet effective and harmonizing in many ways. Within the context of each organization, these apparently conflicting signals were not seen as confusing but were well understood and widely accepted. Staff members interpreted them as different positions that taken as a whole were not in opposition. Instead, the differences provided balance and unity. Rather than canceling out or undermining each other, the contradictions supported, sustained, and complemented one another; they took the form of paradox. By embracing the paradoxical nature of their work and by blending multiple messages and roles, a leader addresses contradictions as a way to achieve balance, unity, and harmony.

Bower's work suggests that leaders help people to think, to seek their own answers, and to make decisions within the boundaries of a dynamic continuum. Leaders encourage followers to be spontaneous and orderly, creative and precise, imaginative and factual. They find their own equilibrium to keep themselves on center. Leaders are like benevolent Zen masters, renowned for that impatience with novices who try to become too logical:

A monk asked the master Ts'wu-wei for what reason the Bodhidharma had come from India. The master answered: "Pass me that chin-rest." As soon as the monk had passed the chin-rest, the master whacked him over the head with it. That is all there is to the story. A chin-rest is a board to support the head during long meditation; and the moral of the story is evidently: don't try to reason—meditate. Through meditation and an occasional whack on the head monks

arrive at the meaning of the statement "One in all and
all in one."[12]

Most principals have little time for meditation. Yet they get
whacked in the head all the time by problems and crises. More time
to reflect and create new modes of reflection may provide a pathway
through the puzzles and inconsistencies of the school day. In the
words of Joseph Campbell, "By putting oneself in accord with [the
way]—one's time, one's world view, oneself—one accomplishes the
ends of life and is at peace in the sense of being in harmony with
all things."[13] Furthermore, facing the unavoidable paradoxes of
work through new approaches to school leadership may help principals deal more effectively as work demands increase, complica-
tions multiply, and ambiguities of purpose grow.

Embracing paradox is a way to work toward balance and
harmony. To clarify the idea of paradox and the blending and balancing of work's opposites, we present in some detail a portrait of
one of Bower's subjects, Paul Morris, principal of Oakwood Middle
School. His creative responses to six paradoxes of leadership and the
commingling of multiple roles demonstrate how complexity may
encourage leaders to reflect and create harmony in difficult
situations.[14]

*The paradox of role expectations:* meeting role expectations
requires creating your own. Do what you are told; do what you are
not told.

Work in schools often demands accommodating new expectations. Teachers spoke of feeling in charge of their work and being
able to shape their own roles. The school's media specialist re-
marked, "Mr. Morris lets me do mostly what I want." Morris himself observed, "I look for teachers who see their role as much broader
than I can describe."[15] Teachers purchase their own supplies and do
not submit lesson plans: "Some principals require teachers to turn
in lesson plans every Friday. They never look at them, and if they
do, don't really know what they are looking for. I look at lesson
plans when I visit classrooms. I just can't imagine going through
them in stacks every week."[16]

By contrast, teachers also noted that their responsibilities
were clear-cut. They were held accountable for assigned tasks and

asked to follow specific rules and procedures. Department heads had monthly meetings with the principal, followed by team meetings with their departments.[17] Morris expected them to carry out assigned tasks while constantly searching for new ways of doing what they were assigned.[18]

*The paradox of performance:* it is right to be wrong in order to be right. Mistakes are expected; do it right.

At Oakwood School, mistakes are readily admitted. A teacher related a story about an after-school program that failed: "It was a special program designed to work with eighth graders who are at risk. This means they will probably drop out before they graduate. . . . There were nine students in the program when it began. After two weeks one student was left. . . . I was embarrassed. Mr. Morris called me in and said, 'Mildred, do you know how many programs similar to this haven't made it? We'll think of something else.' We had a long talk and I left his office. I felt as if I hadn't really been a failure."[19]

On another occasion, a physical education teacher was summoned to the principal's office for not teaching an area assigned to him: "I didn't like to teach health; so I just didn't do it. Well, Mr. Morris called me in one time and said, 'Dave, you're not teaching health. Why?' After some discussion I left, and now I am teaching health."[20]

Mr. Morris expects people to do things right, while simultaneously tolerating mistakes. He resolves the apparent contradiction that it is right to be wrong in order to be right.[21]

*The paradox of problem perception:* problems are best solved by allowing them to be problems. Problems are unavoidable; avoid problems.

On the one hand, Morris communicates that problems are normal occurrences to be accepted: "Just don't make a big deal out of problems." On the other hand, he prides himself on avoiding problems related to mandated reforms: "I read all that stuff from central staff and the state, gobs of stuff, and then I decide what I will give to the teachers and what I won't. Some of these guys (references to other principals) get into a lot of trouble—they create their own problems—because they pass things on down rather than deciding what is important and what can be dismissed."[22]

The contradiction between accepting and avoiding problems is a normal part of life at Oakwood.

*The paradox of pride:* pride in being the best comes from knowing that we are not good enough. Be proud to be the best. We *aren't* good enough.[23]

At Oakwood, the teachers and staff speak with a sense of reverence about their high standards and performance. They believe their school to be one of the best in the state. Frequent award ceremonies, plaques, and letters of recommendation reinforce their pride. Each fall a dramatic production celebrates the previous year's accomplishment.

At the same time, the people at Oakwood are constantly looking for new ways to become better. Morris makes this search for improvement very clear: "We couldn't be in the business of education and not want to learn and improve."[24]

*The paradox of control:* by letting go of control, it remains. The leader is in control. The leader does not control.

"Mr. Morris has control of things; he knows his business" is a common perception at Oakwood. In other words, he knows what is going on inside the school and buffers it against external influence. As he puts it, "If I followed every rule that comes across my desk, I would not be here talking to you today."[25]

But in same breath, Morris recognizes that he cannot control most outside influences and relinquishes control inside: "I hire good teachers and then I support them as they work with the children."[26] Control at Oakwood School is in balance; keeping control and letting loose occur simultaneously.

*The paradox of concern:* acting in a caring way may not mean that the leader is always caring. The leader is tender and cares for individuals. The leader is tough and cares about the organization.

Paul Morris exudes a caring, sensitive attitude, but it is supported by clear standards. He obviously cares about teachers, staff members, and students and treats them lovingly and tenderly. At the same time, he is tough. He dismissed a teacher who could not manage a class. He expelled students, one of whom later got in trouble outside. He rearranged schedules that require teachers to change in midyear routines they had enjoyed for a long time.

Instead of giving simplistic signals, Paul Morris sent blended ones. For every statement or action, there was its opposite: "work together, be autonomous"; "think things through, act"; "be cautious, take risks." Bower argues that apparent contradictions brought unity and balance to his organization as well as to those of the other two leaders. Unraveling the puzzles or balancing opposites helped subordinates to maintain a healthy tension between alternatives. These leaders not only saw the possibilities of both yes and no but they acted within their environments in ways that promoted the balance. The pivotal points for these leaders centered on role expectations, performance, problem perception, pride, control, and concern. As they steered their organizations, they balanced the Yin and Yang of the pivot points.[27]

Although none of the three leaders was conscious of it, all three were intuitively in tune with paradoxical thinking: the principle of polarity is not to be confused with ideas of opposition or conflict. Leadership is lived in the dialectic or tension. As Watts writes, "Our overspecialization in conscious attention and linear thinking has led to the neglect, or ignorance, of the basic principles and rhythms of the process [of living], of which the foremost is polarity."[28]

Harmonizing these polarities can become the important work of school leaders.

### Other Paradoxes of Principals' Work

As noted earlier, schools are challenging, ambiguous, and demanding organizations. The vast array of complex tasks, conflicting pressures, and thorny dilemmas creates a constant state of activity.

In addition to those identified by Bower, principals often deal with many other paradoxes of work.

*People don't work for rewards—reward people.* Teachers and staff find their greatest meaning and reward by having students learn and grow.[29] Yet they also respond to formal recognition, informal rewards, and professional support for their hard work and success.

*Plans always must be revised—plan carefully.* Planning is important to building motivation and coordination for a new program or curriculum. But as action is taken, unpredictable surprises and changing situations make evolutionary planning necessary.[30] Developing flexibility can bring stability.

*If you keep changing, you will never get it right—keep changing.* Studies of school improvement point out that schools will be most successful when they are continuously improving, when change occurs within a community of learners.[31] But without stability, it is hard to perfect promising practices. Finding the balance between stability and constant change is achieving unity.

*Coordination is impossible with so many variables—improve coordination.* Schools have become so complex, with so many specializations and subspecializations, that coordination among groups, units, classrooms, and programs seems impossible. But without enough coordination, schools can disintegrate into a chaos of disjointed and conflicting efforts.

*Follow central office directives—be creatively insubordinate.*[32] Maintaining harmony (the absence of conflict) between schools and the central office is important. School principals cannot afford to become such mavericks that they end up transferred, fired, or demoted. Nor can they be so passive that they do not discover ways to bend rules so that the learning needs of children are served. Finding the right combination of the "independent subordinate" and "loyal deviant" is a requisite of the job.

*Educational outcomes are hard to measure—measure them.* Many of the core outcomes of education remain difficult to identify and measure. Yet it is critical to know and to show how well a school is performing. Principals are constantly searching for and developing ways to measure success that satisfies key stakeholders but does not shift attention or energy from other highly important, enduring (if intangible) parts of a school's sacred mission.

*Allocate resources equally—distribute resources where they are needed most.* School leaders must constantly deal with trade-offs between equity (allocating the same resources to everyone) and the demand for quality (investing resources where they will do the most good). The goal is to find a widely shared sense of quality-directed equity.

*Don't change things too fast—change quickly to make a difference.* School improvement invariably creates changes in educational patterns and practices. Principals regularly seek to balance speed and caution in bringing new programs and approaches into the school. Going too fast derails change; going too slowly decreases success.

*Do not make decisions until you have figured it all out—act before you are sure.* Merging leadership and management requires equal parts of action and reflection. Too much action causes plans to go awry; too much thought creates paralysis that prevents actions from ever being taken. Harmony occurs through reflective action and active reflection.

*Delegate to others—if necessary, do it all yourself.* This is one of the core dilemmas of the principalship. The principal must be willing to be out in front, but he or she must also relish following the lead of others. Without these dual roles in tension, leaders will never discover the leadership of followers or demonstrate the leadership that is revealed in following others.

Each of these paradoxes confronts principals every minute of every day. Each suggests the difficulties and opportunities in merging and balancing the technical and symbolic dualities of school leaders' work. How do these paradoxes work in schools? What is the Yin and what is the Yang, and how can the two opposites be balanced or blended?

The Yin and Yang, symbolic and structural, are part of a larger whole. One taps the left part of our brain, the other the right hemisphere. A bifocal principal is able to interweave these roles easily. One set of issues is usually in the foreground; the other provides a backdrop; just as quickly these switch.

This is how technical and symbolic issues play out in schools. When a principal is dealing with goals, it is against a backdrop of cultural values. When a principal is telling a story, it is done in a context of rational activity. A formal memo may also have a second life as a symbol. A ceremony may make a recent restructuring understandable or heal the wounds that reshuffling of roles and relationships may have caused. In sum, bifocal principals are able to view every part of each day through two lenses and use whichever one the occasion requires. In their heads and through their actions, they are able to balance and blend logic and artistry, dancing on the juncture of the two.

In the next chapter, we provide a picture of a bifocal principal in action. Based on observations and interviews with many principals, "Fran Washington" is a composite portrait of the integrated approach to school leadership.[33]

# Chapter Four

# Harmonizing the Calendar

$P$rincipals report, and research substantiates, that their daily agendas are an almost endless series of brief, fragmented, seemingly unrelated human exchanges. The daily discord extends to weeks and months, making it very difficult for a principal to attend to everything that the position requires. With a full plate of technical details and amorphous cultural dilemmas, how does one decide what gets immediate attention and what can be postponed until later? Fran Washington[1] found a way to harmonize the competing demands on her time by attending to technical and symbolic issues simultaneously, uncovering artistic opportunities in minutiae, and finding logical solutions amidst seemingly indecipherable expressive chaos.

The day of Fran Washington begins to take shape before she is awake. This Tuesday's special situations and problems are already starting to germinate. A child is happily dreaming about being made today's VIP for grade 5. Warm feelings permeate her last hours of sleep. A science teacher is up early to mix a special concoction for a third-grade science experiment. Two teachers are about to be immobilized (one because of a real virus; the other finding an excuse for a bad hangover). At school, the internal "engine" that drives the laser printer for the office computer is getting ready to break down at a crucial moment. Eventually, each of these events will combine with the normal daily grind to make Fran's next twelve hours potentially frantic.

At home, Washington arises to shower, eat breakfast, and ready herself. She reviews the day in her head as she gulps her morning coffee. Arriving at school a little before 7 A.M., she finds three calls on the answering machine: two teachers are out with the flu, the assistant superintendent wants some preliminary budget figures for next year, and the PTO President wants a 9:30 meeting to talk about a fundraising project. As her first decisive action of the day, the principal locates two substitute teachers who know the school, the curriculum, and the students and who are certified to teach at the appropriate grade levels. She is confident that they will have the skills and knowledge that help keep instruction moving and classes under control. In addition, she knows the subs are familiar with the school and share its values. Before any certificated teacher is put on the school list, he or she is screened by the principal and a representative group of teachers. Those who are selected as potential substitutes spend a day learning the history and cultural traditions of the school. Only then are they considered fully "certified" to be called upon to cover a class. Fran wants technically competent subs who also know the ropes. Because of her thoroughness, substituting at the school is seen as a privilege. As a result, her calls for temporary duty receive priority.

By eight o'clock, teachers, the school secretary, and various support personnel stream into the small office and gather in the nearby lounge for coffee and conversation and fresh coffeecake made this morning by one of the teachers. This is an important time each day to reinforce collaborative values, share ideas, and gain support (as well as drink coffee). Washington greets and talks with various people, trying especially to connect with those who made specific requests the day before. Usually these concern materials, answers to specific procedural questions, or teachers just wanting some time with the principal. But beneath the surface, other things are going on. The early-morning mingling is also a cultural ritual. Fran makes sure that she herself demonstrates and emphasizes what she expects from teachers. She is always energetic and cheerful. The school's motto is Every Child—A Promise. Each morning, Fran lets teachers know through words and deeds how important this particular instructional day might be to students—especially those from troubled families.

As she moves around, she also tries to "read" today's climate; she takes the social temperature of those adults without whose nurturant skills the positive social climate would collapse. If that fragile support system evaporated, simple interactions would become strained or destructive and Fran's time would be spent dealing with many more conflicts than usual. Her anthropological detective work gathers clues early in the day and pieces them together quickly. So far, so good, today. Everyone seems fairly happy, almost upbeat. Privately, Fran breathes a sigh of relief, as this is not always the case. She has had to face days when things were not so rosy: teachers who had just learned that a college-age daughter did not receive a scholarship, that a spouse was unfaithful, or that a once-supportive parent went to the school board with a complaint. Fran can often read the levels of concern and energy well ahead of anyone else. She knows the history and makeup of her school staff. She tries to adjust her behavior to head off problems, to provide needed infusions of ideas or energy, and to heal the wounds following conflicts. But sometimes there is no way to stem the tide, and she simply stitches the torn social fabric to hold things together temporarily until the day ends.

During the next twenty minutes, Washington talks to eighteen different people, responds to several different requests for information (updates on field trips, questions about next week's cultural arts programs, or what to do with a child who has just thrown up). The phone continues to ring, piling up seven call-back slips from parents, central office personnel, and a teacher whose child's stomach flu struck on the way to school. The school secretary just received a return call from the local veterinarian. He had received a panicked call from one of the school's teachers. The first grade's gerbil has eaten her new offspring, and one student was visibly distraught. The veterinarian offered some medical advice about the first problem but also noted that his expertise was limited to dealing with animals.

In the midst of this flurry of activity, Fran tries to answer questions and solve problems while simultaneously picking up new information from conversations, nonverbal messages, and asides. In each brief encounter, Fran is also conscious of opportunities to reinforce the values and beliefs of the school. She constantly stresses to the school secretary or anyone who answers the phone the importance of making a good first impression. Every caller is treated as a special client, and every call is treated seriously—even if the matter seems fairly trivial. To Fran, every encounter presents an occasion for sending cultural signals about what the school stands for.

As students begin to arrive, an outwardly unruffled principal moves toward the closet to get her coat. She needs to be outside to greet students, talk to parents who are dropping off their young, and monitor the bus driver about whom she has received a couple of parental complaints. While maintaining control, ensuring the safety of students, and keeping the traffic moving, Fran is also aware of her visibility and the ways that her deeds and demeanor send important cultural messages. She asks students whether they have done their homework, inquires about what they will be learning today, and asks specific questions about the lessons she knows were covered the day before. Her smiles, touches, and hugs let everyone know that the school is also a supportive place where student needs are met. She gives special attention to students who arrive at school obviously unhappy, frustrated, or scared. She ruffles the hair of one, comments on the new Miami Dolphins shirt of another, asks about another's brother who was hurt in an accident, and tosses a Nerf football back to a fourth while complimenting him about his recently displayed math homework. Knowing the names of all the students is not easy, but it demonstrates that she knows who they are and cares about them. These early-morning encounters draw on several technical and symbolic roles: analyst, symbol, actor, potter, poet—often occurring simultaneously within a single encounter.

The arrival of students is also a key time to connect with parents and community members. Washington fields queries from parents about the new math program that does not use a textbook, flags down a retiree who lives nearby to see if he is still being bothered by kids walking across his flowerbeds, and guides a new parent to the main office so that she can fill out school transfer forms. As Fran Washington is taking care of all this, she is constantly articulating the school mission through her words, phrases, metaphors, and stories and gathering more clues about what is currently going on with families and community residents.

As she answers questions, she is simultaneously taking the pulse of the mood of the students today. Their energy level and emotional orientation (positive or negative) will determine in large part the flow of the day. Fran knows how to analyze and interpret the subtle signs. When energy levels are low, conflict will be more intense in the afternoon (she will have to adjudicate more conflicts in her role as jurist). When emotional orientations are negative, there will be greater social discord, less time for instructional tasks, and more students sent to the office for a "talk" with the principal. Knowing the social climate ahead of time will help anticipate the problems and ensure that she will use her own time wisely. She is well aware that her predictions of what lies ahead may not pan out. Even among the best principals, making this early-morning forecast is like predicting the weather; they can increase their accuracy, but they will never be 100 percent on target.

Fran watches as students walk, stroll, and march into their classes. She lingers behind to pick up an abandoned glove and a small trinket that belongs to one of the school's emotionally volatile students. If Fran can return it to the boy immediately, it may save the teacher an hour or more of trying to calm and reassure the youngster. She also recognizes that returning the belongings will demonstrate to the teacher and other students the value of caring about others. On her way to the classroom, the principal is stopped by a parent (who is also a school board member). The parent has a question about a new student assessment system that relies on portfolios of student work instead of standardized tests. Fran's answer is clear, articulate, and consistent with school values. Through a well-chosen metaphor, the parent seems to understand the idea of portfolios better.

## Morning

The tempo of Fran Washington's morning does not slow once classes begin. She spends a good deal of the morning visiting classes, talking with teachers, or observing student work. She sees these actions as both supervision and ritual. The morning is also spent on the telephone contacting parents, returning calls, and disseminating information to superiors, district staff members, and others. She uses the morning to accomplish many of the routine administrative tasks required by federal, state, and local district policies. She often wishes that her retirement salary could be based on a dollar for each form she has filled out over her career. But she knows that fulfilling these tasks on time sends important signals to the outside world. In fact, the excellent external image of the school gives it more latitude and freedom than many other district schools.

As she works on these administrative details, her concentration is often interrupted by parent demands (she talks to an irate parent who wants his child moved immediately to another class), medical problems (a child has broken her arm, and the parents cannot be reached), or budget requests (will there be an additional $250 for science materials this year?). Though not all the interruptions are serious, the principal must deal carefully with each one. For the other person, what is important is solving the problem. But each encounter presents an opportunity to communicate and strengthen school values and beliefs. Combining these two different objectives has become almost second nature to Washington. Blending the technical and symbolic sides of her role as principal has also helped pull her school together into a productive, cohesive social unit.

Fran reserves the morning hours to conduct formal observations of teachers. The instructor whom Washington will be observing this morning poses a pleasant challenge: this is one of the best teachers she has ever seen. The preobservation conference later that morning ranges widely from instructional methods to new curricular materials on higher-order thinking. Fran has done her homework and is able to keep up her side of a very profound dialogue about educational practice. She is able to share ideas with the teacher and to help her tie these to the mission of the school. Fran is well aware that formal supervision is also a symbolic act. As an important ritual, it joins Fran and the teacher together as professionals and bonds them to the school's values and beliefs. It helps to build a shared cultural web in what otherwise might become isolated classrooms with each individual teacher pursuing his or her own personal objectives. After the follow-up conference, Fran feels that she has been helpful. The teacher has learned something from the feedback and obviously appreciates that Washington knows and cares about instruction.

During the morning, Fran also coordinates (and acts as a buffer against) the myriad of outside vendors, salespeople, and voluntary organizations who want to either sell or donate resources to the school. This seemingly simple task is complicated by the fact that some of the vendors are parents or community members and some of the donations are inappropriate or unconstitutional (free Bibles for everyone). Her gatekeeping role has both technical and symbolic sides. Who comes in or is denied access can either cause or solve problems and in addition sends important cultural messages.

In the midst of the morning's fully packed agenda, Fran has a multitude of short meetings with grade chairpersons, custodial staff, school improvement teams, special education "M" teams, and central office administrators and other principals, as well as community groups. Most of these meetings are problem-solving events. Across the meetings, various efforts are integrated as the principal plays a vital coordination link among various players. The meetings also provide occasions for telling stories, bonding, and reinforcing cultural values. For example, in one meeting devoted to textbook selection, Washington moves the discussion to an examination of school values and beliefs that need to serve as a template for the decision. She tells the story of an African-American student who several years ago burst excitedly into her office to show her the picture of an African-American business woman in the new textbook; this was a way of reminding people that textbooks are sources of cultural signals as well as of information. Taken together, these face-to-face exchanges keep the principal up to date, help foster school-community relationships, solve problems before they become acute, and coordinate the activities of a wide range of diverse people into a well-integrated instructural effort. As rituals, the meetings provide occasions for humor, storytelling, and knitting people together into a cultural tapestry.

## Afternoon

Washington's afternoon is often even more filled with conflicts and problems than was the morning. Her best skills at resolving conflicts are called on even before the morning ends. Before the noon hour, energies wane, and patience wears thin on the part of both students and staff. The lunchroom encloses the now-revived high-energy level of many students into a small space. Hundreds of previously confined youngsters see the lunchroom as more than a place to eat. It is also a place to frolic, fight, and plan how to see friends during the afternoon classes.

Whether in the lunchroom or not, Washington is viscerally aware of hundreds of small engines being refueled at once. She knows from previous experience that anything can happen. When rain or inclement weather require students to remain inside after lunch, the potential for conflict increases considerably. During the lunch hour, Fran is highly visible. Just her presence seems to keep everything under control. She responds instantly to mediate disagreements before they erupt into full-scale conflagrations. As she moves from student to student, group to group, she asks questions about the morning lessons. She compliments students on their good behavior, frowns at those who violate the well-known mores of the school, and is constantly hugging or patting students on the head.

After lunch, the principal wedges administrative activities into small niches of time that open up between other duties. This afternoon the district maintenance crew is coming to determine whether reroofing the school can wait a year. Washington will press for the original schedule since her most supportive and creative teacher has a classroom where regular leaks dampen student work displayed on the walls. She will invoke the well-known commitment of the school to exemplary instruction to counter the maintenance supervisor's arguments about competing district priorities. Very soon, the story of her strong-willed insistence and the presence of the roofing crew at the school the next day will be circulated among the teachers who now have added evidence of their principal's heroism.

The president of the school advisory council has also scheduled a visit. She hopes to garner the principal's support in selling holiday paper and cards in November. Washington is worried since there is a vague district policy restricting schools in the display or use of any religious symbols during holidays. Even more important, she is concerned about undermining the school commitment to cultural diversity. She will invoke this value to support her counterproposal that a group of representatives from all ethnic groups in the school plan an ecumenically focused celebration about religion and values. Finally, a local folksinger is due to arrive for an all-school assembly featuring songs supporting conservation of natural resources. These three activities are the scheduled events around which other work must be fitted in.

There is a lot going on. The afternoon also has its litany of unscheduled meetings (about how to replace the refrigerator in the teacher lounge), sudden deadlines (the assistant superintendent needs a list of all students speaking Southeast Asian dialects), and unexpected but common crises (two children have thrown up in their classrooms with the stomach flu that is now spreading; a printer at another school must be found to get a report in on time; the lead teacher on the school improvement team comes in to report she is pregnant; and a joyful medley of children want to show Fran their recent composition or drawing). Every event, no matter how small, has both technical and symbolic components. All require Fran's bifocal attention and balanced responses.

After-school meetings continue, with the faculty gathering to discuss upcoming staff in-service days, the budget for next year, new positions, and the design of the school logo. In these meetings, information is disseminated, problems are solved, and activities are coordinated. But they are also times for creating, reinforcing, and modifying existential commitments. The conversations about the school logo are especially significant, since the logo no longer fully represents what the institution stands for. Many of the problems raised in these after-school meetings have simple technical solutions (find the purchase order forms to have the printer repaired), whereas others have more complicated requirements (finding the best set of materials for the new math project). Each technical activity has its important, symbolic side; for example, responding to a teacher's request to produce a student-written play for the entire school com-

municates the importance of creativity and student initiative. Other
decisions have an even more powerful symbolic impact (the values
the principal conveys when coping with a mediocre teacher who has
not been living up to the curricular standards of the school and may
be asked to move to another school). In small and large ways, Fran
Washington's day is dedicated to solving technical problems and
dealing with the administrative routines of the school while also
reading, shaping, and strengthening the underlying culture of the
school. Each routine communicates some value or norm, and each
symbolic act serves to move formal action along. These dual ends
are inextricably merged in each action, word, and decision of the
school day.

### Longer Cycles

The daily work of principals is chock full of problems, puzzles, and
paradoxes. But a principal's work also has longer cycles. The mix
of challenges varies across weeks, seasons, years, and decades. These
longer cycles require even more sophisticated understanding and
complex versions of the ongoing technical and symbolic roles. As
the portrait of Washington continues, we see how over longer time
spans her roles direct the flow of work and shape the culture of the
school.

### A Week in the Principal's Life

Weeks produce different and even more varied opportunities and
challenges than do days. The week is bounded by weekends, times
when teachers and children alternately rest or party and play too
hard. In the former case, they will show up Monday ready to go. In
the latter, they will arrive already thinking about going home or
simply surviving. The school week itself inexorably uses up the
strength of teachers and students as they engage in learning, playing, and fighting. By week's end, even those who came in recharged
are finding their energy depleted.

Washington's Mondays often see a weary crew of people returning to the challenges of teaching. As the week begins, she must
radiate commitment and vitality. Other Mondays bring a burst of

ideas and energy as people enter the building anxious to bargain and negotiate for her time, resources, and ideas. Monday mornings lock in times and key appointments for the week. Washington carefully reflects on the number of problematic situations that are coming up, the collection of classroom puzzles that she will be required to decipher.

Wednesday is "hump" day—further discussion of the school mission statement, decisions on how to use profits from the soda machine (well over $2,000), and the meeting with the assistant superintendent to lobby for an additional teacher after the holiday break. She thinks about ways to conserve some time on Wednesday so that she will have the energy and focus for the Thursday agenda. The end of the week sees the problems that develop as energies ebb and tempers flare. It is also time to recognize the special accomplishments of the week. Washington has purchased a popcorn popper for the school; each Friday just before the teachers leave, she pops a batch. As teachers gather around the popcorn, they share stories and experiences.

A week in a principal's life is like a white-water river: the width is known, the rocks at various places are charted, and the length is unvarying. What does change is the depth and speed of the water, the ways that the school deals with unexpected turbulence, and the energy level of the paddlers in bow and stern as they work their way through the narrows and past Devil's Drop. The purpose of the voyage also varies. Sometimes it is to reach some distant marker; other times it is to learn to steer; and still other times the journey is made for the simple joy of the challenge.

Similarly, with the school week, there are certain clear and consistent parameters: the number of days, the schedule of classes, and anticipatable problems on Mondays and Fridays when transitions into and out of school produce difficulties. But the course of the actions, feelings, and demands is different each week; staff members' and students' energy, excitement, and motivation rise and fall in unique patterns. Thus, the week involves keeping the boat moving roughly downstream, coordinating the rowers, and maintaining the excitement, the sense of purpose and focus. Coping means knowing the underlying structure of the week—where the rocks and turns are—as well as being ready for unplanned situations and demands; problems grow and become more complex. Washington tries to predict when issues or illness will begin to decrease the precision of steering. At week's end, the principal will be expected to comment on the accomplishments, contributions, and meaning of the journey to parents, teachers, and students. The way that Washington handles both routine and unexpected events not only helps maintain a rational, goal-directed flow of work and energy but also communicates what is important, valued, and expected in the school culture.

### Seasons in a Principal's Life

A principal's day is marked by bells, emergencies, bureaucratic necessities, and whatever the collective mood in the school happens to dictate. Each day of the week presents a different set of routine or vexing challenges. To a veteran principal, many of these events in the weekly calendar are foreseeable (though the unexpected also occurs).

An experienced principal develops the ability to forecast events that extend beyond the day or week. The seasons of the year also produce a flow of behavior.[2] Month by month, every principal must accept new additions to the already clogged daily and weekly agenda. Opening day, Passover, Halloween, the first snow, the holiday season, Valentine's Day, spring break, May Day, Cinco de mayo, and the last day of school—seasonal fluctuations bring a new collection of predictable joys or headaches. The climate of schools and the moods of students, teachers, and principals are heavily influenced by the seasons and rhythms of the year.[3] There is little a principal can do to counteract the effects of these cyclical events. They come and go, marking the passage of time and requiring the principal's response.

The seasons spawn a number of specific problems and dilemmas. Opening day sometimes means a long line of concerned parents, frightened children, and buses that are not on time. Halloween provides teachers and students some welcome relief from instructional tasks but also occasions calls from parents complaining about the school's endorsement of the devil's workshop (All Saints' Day). The first heavy snowfall ensures that parents will telephone at night to find out whether or not school will open the next day. Whereas the holidays once unified the school around shared rituals and pageantry, the season now creates divisive dilemmas because of the range of ethnic groups.

The second semester finds the principal fighting the "blahs," preparing the school improvement plan, and developing the budget collaboratively with parents and staff members. Spring vacation provides another seasonal interruption in the instructional regularity and a chance to recharge for the final months. The last day of school sees discipline problems or tears as students depart now-beloved classes. Boxing up, organizing, and writing the final reports of June intrude on the reflections about the year past. It is time to plan, analyze, and celebrate. Retirements, end-of-year parties, and transfers to other schools are powerful events that end the year and call on the poet and actor roles of the principal.

But summer brings a new set of tasks to the fore as the principal and staff plan, develop a curriculum, arrange schedules, and undergo more professional training. Fran's skills as poetic visionary are needed when the planning committee gets frustrated and wants to decide and get it over with rather than develop a school improvement plan that is closely linked to the school mission.

The ebb and flow of trends in schools creates cyclical issues that affect the work of principals like Fran Washington and others. Daily, weekly, monthly, and yearly, principals are confronted with problems, puzzles, and paradoxes that must be overcome rather than overlooked. The tasks and the meanings attached to every decision, communication, and action by principal and other school leaders move the rational processes along at the same time they build less obvious cultural patterns.

### Mingling Roles in Five Arenas: A Closer Look

Five areas (bus duty, the school tour, faculty meetings, parent conferences, and textbook selection) are particularly crucial in shaping the course of work and the deeper features of school culture. These will receive more detailed attention to remind us that seemingly inconsequential activities can serve important technical and symbolic purposes.

## Bus Duty

For Fran, as we have already seen, bus duty has important technical aspects. She keeps young charges under control, ensures their safety, and makes sure that everyone gets on the right bus or is released to an official parent or guardian.

Bus duty is also an important event that daily shapes school culture. These early-morning greetings and late-afternoon goodbyes are important rituals of reconnection, communication, and bonding. Being at the bus stop when children arrive or leave provides an opportunity for Washington to talk with students whose deportment has been less than pleasant as well as those who seek her smile for accomplishments present or past.

In the bus area, she assesses the social climate, reinforces norms and values, and broadcasts the passion and purposes of the school. In one short period, Washington might ask one child about his homework, muss the hair of another while asking about a sick parent, find out about the most recent popular cartoon and song, or identify students experiencing hard times at home.

While these activities collect data, coordinate schedules, and solve conflicts, they are also highly symbolic. Her appearance, the things she appreciates or scolds, and the nature of her greetings or goodbyes demonstrate what the school believes in. To parents, seeing the principal in action reassures them that their children are in good hands. As a symbolic activity, bus duty can reinforce such values as concern for individual students, the importance of homework, and the idea that caring and helping are part of the school's way of life. Fran never misses an opportunity to ask students about their homework or to inquire about how things are at home. Talking with a teacher, student, or parent at the day's beginning or end gathers important information, orchestrates small celebrations of achievement, welcomes new members to the school, and reinforces school traditions.

## The School Tour

Washington tours her building on a regular basis. A walk through a school can be a simple act of supervision, like a warden touring

a maximum security prison to keep people on task and in line. For
Fran, walking around serves many interlocking purposes. On the
one hand, she is gathering information about the physical plant,
teacher activity, student engagement, and the performance of the
instructional program. On the other hand, she is communicating
and reinforcing the symbolic glue that holds the school together.

What she notices, recognizes, applauds, or questions is carefully monitored for its symbolic content. She molds language, symbols, and artifacts at the same time that she is overseeing the
progress of teaching and learning. Shaping culture and identifying
social and physical conditions that need maintenance or caring attention are intertwined.

By observing teaching on the fly, Washington sees how the
school curriculum is being presented; how well teachers, students,
and other staff are working together; and what the quality of student academic work is. Seemingly small comments are important
indications about how goals are being achieved, what can be improved, or what future new directions might be taken—how far a
new vision can go.

A tour also provides a way to shape the culture of the school.
At the same time that she is gathering information or solving routine problems, she sends culturally relevant signals about what is
valued, what actions or orientations are preferred, how professionals and parents should be treated, and what language to use in
describing unruly students. The fact that Fran is visible in the hallways, libraries, and classrooms communicates that the world of students, teachers, and staff members matters.

### Faculty Meetings

Faculty meetings help coordinate diverse efforts into a harmonious
schoolwide program. Meetings also provide important ritual exchanges that connect people to each other and to their shared mission. Washington, aware of this dual nature of meetings, speaks
intensely of student learning and social development; she carefully
recognizes (so as not to embarrass or overwhelm) the special
contributions of innovative teachers while consciously avoiding

alienating the small group that is resisting new instructional approaches.

Faculty meetings are a boon and a bane among Washington's duties. She knows that these regular times for gathering can provide opportunities for sharing new information as well as a chance to strengthen a common sense of meaning, purpose, and accomplishment. During faculty meetings, Fran and her staff share stories of success and failure and pass along ideas that might be useful to their colleagues. Making meetings like clan gatherings, she encourages rituals of reconnection (breaking bread together, sharing fears and hopes, distributing useful readings), poetically restates what makes the school special, and invests actions, decisions, and activities with meaning and value.

### Parent Conferences

Parent conferences, dreaded events in some schools, are welcomed and applauded in Washington's school. Parents and teachers alike share the joys and accomplishments of students, while pinpointing and discussing areas for improvement. To make these conferences successful, Washington connects them to student dramas and performances, presentations about parenting, or ceremonies to recognize student or teacher accomplishments.

She knows that these large gatherings serve important technical ends. During the awards assembly, for example (which incidentally draws most school parents), Washington carefully collects data about common parent concerns, disseminates information about upcoming student events, and describes the new science program.

She also is fully aware of what the event means symbolically. Constantly, she is emphasizing what the school holds dear. The intonation of her voice itself radiates pride as she tells stories about new programs, extols dedicated teachers, and describes her vision for an exciting future. These events knit parents and community residents into the cultural fabric of the school. They are a bonding experience that give everyone a chance to celebrate what the school is all about. Students have the chance to share what is special about the school with their parents. Teachers have the opportunity to brag about student work and show all their own professional skills. Parents have the opportunity to reconnect with and reminisce about their own school experiences.

Washington makes routine events serve both informational and social purposes. Parent conferences disseminate data, but at the same time they reinforce a belief in the importance of meeting and of developing a shared purpose. An awards night communicates information about what the school does at the same time that it builds organizational pride. Washington shapes her school by interweaving symbolic and technical matters into vibrant and meaningful parental events.

### Textbook Selection

Selecting textbooks and other materials can be an afterthought. In Washington's case, it is a key technical decision that must support school educational values. The selection of teaching materials, especially textbooks, has always been an important and enervating process. Now that Washington's school is using more supplementary materials and fewer textbooks, the process of decision making has become a significant aspect of cultural reinforcement. Discussions about textbooks are peppered with references to shared educational beliefs and values. Course purposes are reviewed and revised, as needed. The content and delivery of instruction are reexamined for criteria that will influence decisions about which materials will work best. In these selection meetings, Washington insists on a collaborative decision process. At the same time, she presses the staff to examine and recommit to or revise deeper beliefs and educational values that will carry the school forward. Thus, decisions about textbooks identify appropriate instructional resources while simultaneously providing a forum for deeper discussions of educational values, beliefs, and purposes.

The decision about what textbooks to purchase (or whether to purchase them at all) is governed by and governs teachers' beliefs about instructional content and methods. Pedagogic materials are the tools that teachers rely on as they help children learn. Materials are also symbols that represent the educational commitments of a school. The topics discussed as teachers select their tools define the level, quality, and focus of teaching and learning in the school. Will students use trade books or a traditional reading series? Should higher-order thinking be a central component for all students? How much drill and practice will be encouraged? These and other questions are crucial in schoolwide decisions about textbooks or other instructional materials.

Washington does not treat these decisions as simple technical exercises. She also sees them as cultural ceremonies and rituals of professional dialogue. Over time, her teachers have used, abused, loved, and hated their textbooks. Nonetheless, parting with these old tools is not always easy. Washington knows that the selection of a new textbook must be marked as a key event in the curricular and cultural history of the school. Old textbooks are ritually packaged and sent to needy schools or given to others who could use them. One copy is kept and displayed with others in a large glass case in the entryway. The school's instructional history is highly visible. Washington sees that stories of the past successes and future hopes are retold to help bridge the transition to new texts and new programs. As a healer and historian, Washington helps diminish the sense of loss and recognizes the prior contributions of the texts.

Fran Washington now realizes that her ability to see and work on technical and symbolic planes simultaneously has added immeasurably to her professional impact. Her blending of these planes also helps to ensure that her school is a meaningful and beloved institution as well as a goal-directed, well-coordinated enterprise that lets teachers teach, students learn, and parents feel confident that their most prized possessions are in capable hands.

# Chapter Five

# The Balanced School

Competing images are not only embedded in conceptions of leadership. They are also reflected in our assumptions about the purpose and design of schools. Here again, two main images predominate, each with a different angle: one rational, the other symbolic. Two metaphors help to illuminate the seeming differences between the two. The first depicts schools as well-run factories; the second envisions them as beloved cathedrals or temples.[1]

The factory image, as the metaphor suggests, focuses on results, outputs, structures, and roles. The main concerns are student control and academic achievement—usually measured in very specific terms. This view assumes the need for a tightly organized and technically focused school where the attention of everyone is centered on explicit, measurable goals and objectives. Participants know what they are supposed to do, and are rewarded when they do well; if they do not, they are given specific suggestions about how they can improve. People know how their efforts relate to others and who is in charge of what. This way of looking at schools emphasizes the importance of managing their technical mission: instruction.[2]

In contrast, the school-as-temple image sees the primary issue as faith—maintaining the spiritual confidence of important constituents and ensuring that the institution is a meaningful, valued endeavor. Attention focuses on the expressive, symbolic aspects of a school. Cultural patterns and practices are expected to be internally cohesive and consistent with values and beliefs of a local community. This conception embraces the importance of values, commitment, passion, vision, and heart—key ingredients of a beloved institution. Managing roles, structures, and outcomes takes a secondary role to maintaining community confidence and faith in the entire enterprise.[3]

In Table 5.1, the organizational characteristics that each metaphor suggests are contrasted.

The symbolic view of schools favors a loosely organized institution, knit together by deeply held organic bonds that help maintain faith and purpose. In contrast, the technical view champions a more conventionally organized institution, held together by fairly applied authority and rules and accountable for achieving specific results. Tension between these two images causes a good deal of disagreement among policy makers, professional educators,

**Table 5.1 Competing Images of School as Organizations.**

| Key Focus | Technical Results | Symbolic Faith and Meaning |
|---|---|---|
| Goals | Clear and measurable | Multiple, diffuse, conflicting |
| Nature of technology | Known connection between means and outcomes | Complex, nonlinear connection between means and ends |
| Roles | Clear and well defined | Unclear, fluid |
| Prevailing logic | Rationality | Spirituality, inspiration |
| Coordination | Routine, mechanical | Organic, loose |
| Environment | Stable, certain, economic exchange | Turbulent, unclear, symbolic exchange |
| Control systems | Explicit, primarily commands or rules | Implicit, primarily values and norms |
| Authority | Hierarchical | Moral |

and interested laypeople about how well schools are doing, what principals should do, and how learning might be improved.

## Problems of Each Conception

In reality, this polarizing debate pulls schools in two different directions without much hope of reconciliation. This situation creates the same dilemma for the design of school as it does for principals who are trying to figure out their personal leadership styles. Each of the contrasting conceptions has strong points but each also has its deficiencies. Overly technical schools can produce results but often lack clear values, strong commitment, and broad support. Deeply beloved schools can be meaningful, value-driven communities that nevertheless fail to produce tangible outcomes. Table 5.2 shows the different problems that schools organized solely around one of these metaphors or another might experience.

Can this dichotomy be resolved? Can the sharp distinctions of these dualities be merged? Here again, we need to move beyond our dualistic either-or thinking to create schools that are meaningful "factories" as well as productive "temples." Though this undertaking may prove difficult, we think that maintaining such a balance and harmony is well within the grasp of any school—if people can attend to both technical and symbolic challenges. Principals can find possibilities for finding value-shaping drama within routines while also inventing novel ways of making drama functional. Tomorrow's schools balance and harmonize technical and symbolic aspects in dynamic equilibrium and constant interplay.

## Dramatic Routine

Today's schools are filled with hundreds, if not thousands, of daily, weekly, and yearly routines. From the collection of lunch money in the morning to the last bus out at night, the flow of functional activity fills the school day. These activities are not merely mechanistic actions completed by programmed robots. They also signal values and cultural norms. In their form and function, they communicate and reinforce a complex mix of values and educational beliefs. Take the morning exercise at Caldwood Elementary School

Table 5.2. Pitfalls of a Single Conception of Schools.

| Technical | Symbolic |
|---|---|
| Means become ends. | Ends-goals are ignored or not stressed. |
| Work becomes routine. | Ritual replaces work. |
| People do only what is required. | People do only what is fun. |
| Commitment to the organization is minimal. | Overattachment to organization is common. |
| Tangible rewards become prime motivator. | There is overreliance on symbolic motivation. |
| There is too much focus on short term, preoccupation with results, and loss of big picture. | There is overemphasis on long-term vision; important details are overlooked. |
| Attention to parts supplants the whole. | Whole overwhelms the parts. |
| Creativity is minimized. | Control is undermined. |
| Membership is ephemeral. | Membership is addictive. |
| The relationship with the community is primarily economic; we will supply resources if you provide outcomes. | The relationship between the community and school is contingent on common values and beliefs. |

in Texas as an example. The principal has made what at other schools is often a perfunctory, technically oriented beginning into an inspired cultural ritual:

> Our morning exercises are really very simple: we usually have a child lead us in the pledges to the American and Texas flags, a patriotic song such as the "Star Spangled Banner" or "America the Beautiful" and our school song (I wrote the words and we use an old tune). I make announcements and sometimes stress the code of honor, our motto, or a school cheer. "What's the first word in our code of honor?" We will "treat others like we want to be treated!" The student leader, at times, will instruct the students to repeat the code of honor after me. I will often ask "What's our

motto?"—"Catch the spirit of learning at Caldwood!"
their thunderous voices respond. On some days, we do
a cheer such as "We're the number one school and
we're the best at reading and writing and all the rest!
We love our teachers, they make our day. Three cheers
for us, hip, hip, hurray!" [Dr. Sally Blewett, letter to
the author, 1990].

Thus, technical activity often plays a powerful expressive, symbolic
role in schools. These functional activities serve as carriers of cultural messages and expectations well beyond what they accomplish.
In the following examples, we show how routines in schools become important carriers of the culture.

### Budgeting as a Statement of Values

Developing a budget is often viewed as simply a formal process of
rationally allocating resources to priority goals and activities. This
process makes good sense. External agencies and constituencies require careful and prudent fiscal accountability. Budgets support
investments in different parts of a school and also act as a formal
planning device to coordinate varied efforts of individuals and
groups.

But spending plans also communicate values, beliefs, and
expectations. Funding allocations signal what is important and
what is valued by putting resources one place or another. In one
high school, for example, the principal and school steering committee provide additional funds for computers and staff development
for departments that are working to implement new learning tech-
nologies. The display of additional resources makes concrete the
school's stated commitment to technology.

Budgets also demonstrate trade-offs that ought to be made
among competing values. At John Muir School, for instance, the
staff and administration decided to decrease class size in early grades
and increase it in later grades to give at-risk students more assistance. This action reinforced the school commitment to serving students who were performing at the margin and who might eventually drop out.

Allocation decisions redirect emphasis from the importance of the instructional process (providing opportunities to learn) to the importance of learning outcomes (ensuring that students have learned what is taught). One school site council asks of each request for money, textbooks, materials, or supplies, "What student outcomes will these purchases foster, and are these the most important outcomes to pursue?" This practice reinforces the belief that student learning is the most important pathway to building a quality school.

Budgetary decisions, especially when part of a school improvement effort, can reshape basic assumptions about problem solving and change. Allocating assets to programs or personnel signals that leaders and staff believe that problems can be analyzed, that professionals can develop better alternatives, and that resources properly placed can make a difference.

The budgeting process also communicates beliefs about power and authority. The decision to involve staff members in making important budgetary decisions says a lot about their respective value and influence. In one school, teachers submit a list of requests to the principal, who then deletes anything that she does not want purchased. This allocation process reinforces traditional beliefs about the authority of principals over teachers. In another school, a different set of beliefs is communicated. There the school council meets collaboratively to review funding requests and to develop a tentative budget; the council then submits it to the faculty for final approval. School beliefs about cooperating, sharing power, and working together are strengthened as a result.

### Planning as a Cultural Event

Planning helps to identify future goals, roles, rules, and responsibilities. Planning is also an effective means of coordinating efforts among teachers, staff members, departments, and grade levels. But planning is also an expressive, symbolic activity. Attending to the symbolic side of planning is a powerful way to shape and solidify school culture.

The deep symbolic meaning and messages of the planning approach can build powerful norms of collegiality ("we share ideas and support"), performance ("we work hard here"), and improvement ("we are always looking for better ways to do things").[4] Or planning can contribute to the contrasting norms of individualism ("we work alone"), mediocrity ("we work hard enough"), and inertia ("we don't need to improve, we're good enough"). Planning communicates the values of collaboration and shared governance. It can also develop a sense of history and identification with the school.

In a midwestern elementary school, the planning process is a highly collaborative activity. Each year, the school improvement team identifies areas that need attention. The team meets at a local university for an intense ten-hour-a-day, weeklong planning effort to develop programmatic suggestions for the coming year. It brings the group together in a retreat setting where shared values are developed and reinforced or where they are modified and commitment is developed. The activity forms deep bonds among the faculty. Stories of previous retreats are a source of humor and a vivid reminder of what the school stands for.[5]

In a southern high school, the principal and staff meet each summer in a hotel to discuss how well the school is performing, to plan new programs, and to share ideas about possible redesign options. Discussions continue long into the night. The principal, teachers, and other staff members discuss wide-ranging ways of how to restructure the school and instructional methods. As everyone eats and plays together, tight connections are formed, and evolving values and rituals help to ensure a cohesive culture that will support the restructuring efforts. The planning process itself is an organic activity that may ultimately transform the school.[6]

In still another school, the planning group travels together to conferences in vans. These trips provide occasions for reflection and long discussions about the nature of teaching and learning. The principal realizes that the stories, the rituals, and the informal by-products of attending the conference are probably more important than the event itself.

Planning, like other routine activity, provides symbolic signals in its form and function. Planning provides a rich crucible of human activity in which cultural values are invented, reinforced, or transformed and group identity is created.[7] Planning also signals to external constituencies that the school is looking ahead and making preparations for the future. Their faith and confidence in the school are maintained in the process.

### Supervision as Cultural Reinforcement

Supervision serves several technical purposes: quality control, coordination, and feedback for on-the-job improvement. Yet supervision has also been characterized as a ceremonial activity, shaping underlying cultural patterns and practices.[8]

First, supervision supports a belief in the existence of a relevant knowledge base in teaching. Supervisors are assumed to have acquired knowledge through prior experience that can be transmitted to novices. Second, supervision encourages the idea that teaching and instruction can be analyzed or broken down into understandable component parts and transmitted as craft knowledge. Third, supervision communicates through nonverbal messages specific ideas for improving teaching and normative assumptions about instruction and student learning. Fourth, supervision serves as an important ritual; it bonds teachers with exemplary role models and the values of their profession. Finally, supervision provides an opportunity for the sharing of stories, metaphors, and other linguistic forms that carry and reinforce intangible cultural archetypes, images, and implicit values.

In one Louisiana school, teachers regularly review (at least once a month) each teacher's pedagogy. Through the dialogue that follows, the staff builds consistency across classes, shares valued knowledge, and creates a professional community. Because the process includes everyone in a "supervisory" role, it also strengthens a belief in collegial, rather than bureaucratic, control.[9]

### Hiring as an Initiation Ritual

Hiring is a technical process to select individuals who possess the requisite skills, intelligence, and capacities to serve as competent teachers. The selection also communicates the importance (or lack thereof) of what it means to become a member of the school. The more time and attention paid to hiring, the more employees (as well as the newcomers) perceive themselves as special.

In Cherry Creek High School, under the leadership of Hank Cotton, hiring was a critical part of shaping the culture. Not only did the principal seek individuals who shared the school values of high performance, academic excellence, and continuous improvement, he also used hiring as a way of communicating a commitment to a high-quality staff. He regularly told a story about how he had spent years recruiting the director of the Instructional Materials Center. Hiring practices showed that Cherry Creek High only wanted the best.[10] In a northern Wisconsin school, a principal interviewed over a dozen different applicants to identify the right teacher for the faculty. This action was proof to all members of the faculty that the principal believed in the importance of a top-quality teaching staff.[11]

A second important symbolic feature of hiring is the opportunity that it offers for building a clan. Hiring people who have similar values helps create an internalized form of cultural control. People work hard at the right things because of a shared commitment. Less bureaucratic and hierarchical control is necessary in these kinds of schools. Selecting people who fit the mold is important in promoting cultural cohesiveness. Consciously selecting mavericks with different ideas stimulates cultural change and reinforces the value of encouraging different viewpoints.

### Transfer and Dismissal as Cultural Excommunication

The dismissal of employees is a difficult task for anyone. These tough decisions are usually made after many months of deliberation, documentation, and attempts at remediation. The practice of firing serves important functional ends because incompetent employees make it difficult for other people to work effectively. Think about the third-grade teacher who receives a class of students from an incompetent second-grade teacher. Additionally, nonperforming teachers and other employees lower standards of quality and performance. It does not take many marginal or incompetent people to reduce schoolwide performance on achievement tests or other indicators of quality.

But the act of dismissal has its symbolic side as well. Termination excommunicates those who do not subscribe to important cultural values. Firing an incompetent teacher is a powerful indication of the performance that a culture requires. In any school, everyone knows who the incompetent people are (if any continue in the school). When they are tolerated year after year, it makes it extremely difficult to assert a commitment to quality and pride. In a midwestern high school, a social studies teacher wandered the halls without anything to do. The principal had removed him from the classroom because of his incompetence. But he had not taken the next step—terminating his contract. The fact that the teacher was allowed to hang around the hallways had a major impact on staff morale and community confidence. However, the principal of a southern elementary school counseled a teacher to move to another school when it was clear that outside jobs made it impossible for that instructor to achieve the necessary level of instructional improvement and innovation. The norm of "working 120%" was maintained.[12]

Public excommunication of people who are not serving a student-centered mission is one way a school demonstrates what it values.

### Retirement as Anointing

Retirement has its technical aspects: completing contractual arrangements, replacing personnel, and making sure that the appropriate benefits flow to the retiree. But it also provides an opportunity for showcasing important values.

Retirement under any circumstances is an uneasy and painful process, both for those who leave and those who remain. It involves reliving past experiences, accepting the transiency of life, and ending professional relationships and a lifelong career. Retirement is an important time for healing the hurt and loss of a valued member of the community. It is also a moment for communicating shared values of loyalty, commitment, and caring. Retirements are as important to those who continue on as they are to those who are leaving. The design of a retirement event requires careful, sensitive symbolic attention. It is another solid benchmark in the emerging history of a school.

In an Iowa elementary school, the principal planned a joint retirement for two teachers who had served the school over thirty-five years each. Past graduates from each decade told stories about the retirees. The staff celebrated their dedication and loyalty. As a final gesture, the principal presented to the teachers the doorknobs from the classrooms in which they had taught—mounted on walnut plaques.

Retirement ceremonies—where stories of past accomplishments affirm core values and describe the contributions of the retiring staff member—are a chance to create a community celebration, but only if done honestly and without hidden motives.

### Coordination to Build Cultural Networks

Coordination is important to ensure that events and activities are sequenced properly and efficiently. It minimizes problems of mutual interdependence in the naturally complex world of individuals, class schedules, and materials.

The form that coordination takes says a great deal about what a school values. Vertical coordination, through either command or rules, emphasizes the value of authority and a belief that people in top positions have a better idea than those further down the formal hierarchy about how to get things to work effectively. Lateral coordination supports the value of collegiality and the idea that integration happens best when people can synchronize their activities through face-to-face dialogue and on-the-spot collaboration.

Many schools with site-based management have extra planning periods for teachers to work on governance and planning; these communicate the importance of collaborative coordination. Other schools involve staff members in deciding teacher schedules and sports events. This practice fosters collaboration and a sense of collegiality by tying together staff members across grade levels or subjects.

Collaborative coordination increases the ties between teachers and builds the informal networks of the culture.

## Communication as Cultural Signals

Communication is one of the most important aspects of life in any human organization. Technically, *communication* means distributing information so that everyone knows what is happening, how their work affects others, what new techniques are available, and so forth. Like coordination, communication can take many different forms. Choices about how best to convey information are based as much on values and beliefs about interchanges as on technical criteria of what is most efficient. How school leaders communicate shapes the school culture.

Memos are commonplace items in schools. Memoranda and written documentation provide durable information, promote high degrees of accuracy, and offer a formal audit trail that can sometimes pinpoint where communication breaks down. Memoranda can also imply either a sense of professional collegiality or one of impersonality and the sense that communication is a one-way street. At the same time, embedded in the words and format of memoranda are connections to larger purposes, to collaborative professionalism, and to hopes for the future. For example, memos in one school feature its mission and motto, as well as children's drawings on each page.

In an Alabama school, meetings begin with another kind of communication: a minimum of five stories of success shared by faculty or staff. These stories keep people up to date on what is happening and furnish an arena to celebrate small successes. Many principals communicate the value they place on classrooms and kids when they religiously tour buildings and visit classes every morning to share ideas, provide positive feedback, and pass along information.

Communication can take place in formal meetings or face to face. Face-to-face dialogue is another technically efficient way of passing along information. But unless meetings operate under conditions of openness and trust, these highly time-intensive encounters operate no better than a public reading of verbal memos. Good conversation involves a mutually guided process of advocacy and inquiry in which people listen as well as they speak. Open meetings are a sign of open cultures where signals are collectively sent and interpreted. Face-to-face exchanges, properly constructed, offer crucibles in which shared values are forged and concentrated. To be effective, authentic dialogue between principal and staff requires a value of openness and a belief in the process.

Professional dialogue can be one of the most powerful anchors of a cohesive culture.[13] It reinforces professionalism as an alternative to social distance and isolation. It indicates that the principal is one of the staff, a professional colleague working with teachers rather than governing over them. It can encourage belief in the benefits of direct, personal contact. Finally, it conveys a strong belief in dialogue as a quick and direct way of gathering information and communicating with others.

### Teacher Promotion as Cultural Celebration

The promotion of teachers to tenured status satisfies contractual and statutory requirements. In a technical sense, tenured teachers operate under a different set of legal conditions. Unlike probationary teachers, they are subject to dismissal only through due process and for unique problems. But the granting of tenure has an expressive, symbolic side as well. It marks the transition from novice to expert, a symbolic journey into the sacred profession of teaching and into membership in the school community.

In one northwestern district, teachers go through a legislated tenure process similar to that of other districts. What is different is the way that teachers become officially tenured. In a ceremonial ritual, they are accepted into the district and the profession of teaching. As in a convocation ceremony, teachers are granted their tenure in a festive occasion complete with academic robes, speeches about the values of teaching, and all of the accoutrements of a major and meaningful event.

While still satisfying statutory requirements and contractual agreements, teacher promotion is a way of publicly communicating and reinforcing the important values and beliefs of both the profession and the school district.

### School Closing as Function and Ritual

Schools are usually closed because of safety problems, space needs, or demographic changes. The closing of a school creates enormous technical challenges. Specific criteria guide decisions about which schools to close. Moving from an existing school to a new site requires planning and coordination. Equipment and people must be moved as efficiently and effectively as possible.

The closing of a school is also a powerful cultural experience. Moving to a new school is a wrenching cultural transition. Staff members need to deal with the grief and loss of the old school. Even in a new setting, memories, old stories, and nostalgia still abound. A physical move does not break existential attachments and emotional ties. Finding a way to make the technical logistics of boxing up and moving on a healing transition ritual is a challenge. Properly orchestrated, wakes, funerals, mourning periods, and memorials help people to let go and move on emotionally and spiritually as well as physically.

Even young children seem to realize the importance of marking transitions with ritual. Following a taxpayers' rebellion in Massachusetts, schools were forced to terminate personnel as a way to keep budgets in balance. In one elementary school, five teaching positions were eliminated. The school lost five of its best-liked teachers. One day, the students organized an event to commemorate the departed teachers. They named a different hallway after each of the teachers by posting their names on the hallway walls. Physically the teachers were gone, but the ritual ensured their memory would remain with the school.

### Seasonal Actions as Symbols

Dramatic opportunities arise around all routine events—or annual cycles. Symbolic passages in the academic calendar join people to each other and to their visions and traditions. The opening of school, for example, is an important event. From a technical standpoint, summer plans are put into action, students are assigned to classrooms, and teachers receive the resources and materials they will need to achieve important instructional objectives. But the beginning of school is also an annual transition ritual that sets the tone for the year. It is a time to acculturate new members and show them the ropes. Time is provided for teachers to disconnect themselves from summer vacation and reconnect with each other and with shared professional values that will guide the year's instruction. One West Virginia district hosts a massive celebration of school opening where the focus is on deeper values. Speeches, bands, and hot-air balloons mark the festive transition and convey the importance of everyone's contribution to learning (personal communication with Lydia McCue, director of adolescent education, Winfield, West Virginia, 1989).

Getting started again after vacation or holidays requires special attention; routines and rules must be reestablished, and functional roles, relationships, and authority patterns must be reaffirmed and relinked to the values and philosophy of the school. Moreover, reentry offers an opportunity to reinforce schoolwide values and to remind teachers of their sacred trust.

Vacations also need to be appropriately launched. The school year's end is a particularly powerful cultural event. Healing the loss felt by teachers whose classes were a joy, celebrating goals accomplished, and reflecting on the joys and travails of a year left behind offer a chance to bury the old year but also to celebrate hopes for the future. To mark this event, one school meets after all the administrative details have been completed. People are expected to tell one story of the year that touched them, cheered them, or made them proud. Awards for challenges met (sometimes an army helmet) are presented, and hopes and plans for the coming year are shared.

When activities marking transitions are carried out with their dual (symbolic as well as technical) purpose in mind, an added benefit is achieved with little extra effort. But it does not stop there. In its play, the porpoise prepares for defending itself and getting food. The same is true in all organizations. Expressive, symbolic activity also has functional value. In this section, we focused on "porpoiseful" purpose. In the next, we will look at the other side of the coin: purposeful play.

## Purposeful Play

More often than we realize, our modern way of thinking causes us to conclude that the symbolic side of organizations is all fun and fluff. But this is simply not the case. Just as routine can become ritual, ritual can serve functional purposes. Symbolic activity often produces tangible results, better coordination, and well-functioning schools. Symbols and expressive activity serve as implicit sources of direction, communication, and coordination.

### History as Policy

Policy is usually intended to establish a common course of action or a uniform code of behavior. Even so, most people recognize the gap between the ideal intentions of a policy and its actual consequences. One reason is that historical precedent is at work dictating what people actually do. Echoes of the past sculpture actions of the present more powerfully than we realize. We do not do things because policies say so. We do them because we have always done them that way, because they are part of the unwritten cultural rules. Knowing how things got where they are (knowing the history of the school) is a crucial first step in trying to change behavior.

Recreating or reinterpreting cultural history can have more influence than establishing a formal policy. History, because it establishes informal precedent through tradition, serves as a vital source of unwritten policy.

For example, a principal of a large high school called on older teachers to recreate the three-decade history of the institution for the entire faculty. As the pageant unfolded, members of the group saw how they had drifted far from their original roots and forgotten what they stood for. Actions had become devoid of meaning. Rather than trying to reform the school, the principal was asking them to revive a glorious past.

A middle school that had formerly been a junior high gathered all the trophies, academic awards, old basketballs, and other memorabilia of past successes in a glass display when the school reopened. While emphasizing a certain continuity with the past, this event also helped to put the old times away. The school entryway is now ablaze with student work and its new statement of values—signaling a symbolic statement of what is important now.

Reliving the past successes and challenges can communicate norms of behavior, values, and goals to aspire to as much as any job description or plan can. Yet stories from school history can also connect to deeper wells of purpose and professionalism and help move the culture forward.

### Values as Goals

*Goals,* tangible ends to strive for, are often defined carefully and measured systematically to determine progress over a given time period. *Values,* by contrast, are the intrinsic qualities an organization stands for, what it considers good and important. Values are more intangible, less clearly delineated, and frequently expressed in abstract symbols or metaphorical stories. They can be interpreted in a variety of ways, giving them more elasticity and flexibility than concrete goals. Determining how well an organization is living up to its values is more a subjective than an objective matter. Despite this fact, values often serve as goals to be achieved, ends to be attained.

One middle school's core value, "reaching for excellence," encourages students to excel at whatever they do. School achievement scores have improved significantly since the value was articulated. The principal attributes the rise in scores to a symbolic commitment: "The test scores by themselves were never goals that motivated students to achieve. But our shared commitment to striving for the best performance possible, while not tangible or specific, has made a big difference in what we can accomplish."

Values are communicated in everything a school leader does, writes, and speaks. Consistency in behavior and connection to convictions about student learning and growth serve to mold core values as well as to encourage progress.

### Heroes as Supervisors

Supervision is typically a firsthand, on-the-spot, face-to-face activity. Supervisors observe subordinates and then either provide compliments for a job well done or make suggestions for improvement. Effective supervision requires both direct observation and concrete feedback. Though these are important, there are less tangible forms of supervision that have an implicit, indirect effect on how people do their jobs.

All people have heroes or heroines whom they try to emulate.

People carry images and stories of their human exemplars and often, consciously or otherwise, look to them for direction and guidance. Neither necessarily tangible nor observable, heroes and heroines still exert considerable influence on how principals or teachers go about their daily duties. They function as supervisory ghosts looking over the shoulder to offer advice and suggestions. As one teacher put it, "Even though she'll never know it, Miss Jones is with me every day I teach. She was the best teacher I ever had. In my head, I have conversations with her about how to handle situations. She is a great source of guidance and support even though she's been dead for years." Identifying and recognizing schoolwide educational heroes and heroines is an effective and collegial way of providing an alternative source of supervision.

### Stories as Coordination

Synchronizing diverse efforts is generally accomplished through planning, formal meetings, or hierarchical control. Stories have a similar impact in less formal but no less powerful ways. Stories carry values and archetypes that let everyone know what is expected. The story at one school of how everyone pitched in during a snowstorm is told over and over. To keep students and worried parents calmed down and harried bus drivers in check, everyone helped. Normally, each person did his or her own thing, in isolation. But in order to survive, it was necessary for people to work closely together; there was time for neither planning nor conflict. One step at a time, through mutual adjustments, the faculty and staff got through the crisis without any lost children or irate parents. They found that they could work together informally in a way that was heretofore impossible—even with all their meetings and planning. The story continues the tradition of their cooperation and success.

At another institution, Frank Boyden, the original headmaster of Deerfield Academy, told the story of the superb teacher who chose to stay on staff and thus to forgo a large salary increase offered by another school because he believed in the values of Deerfield.[14] Still another school has discovered that by recounting stories of the collaborative planning and implementation of a teacher-led training conference, new members learned that they were to help out, collaborate, and provide workshops, even if no one formally required them to.

Stories tie staff members to the shared successes of the school and delineate the valued roles they can play. They can also illuminate the puzzles and paradoxes of work.

## Rituals as Rules

Rules regulate behavior in an authoritative way. Rituals do the same thing through implicit understandings of underlying norms and values. Violating a stated rule will result in answering to someone in authority. Failing to follow the correct procedures of an unstated ritual invites social sanctions from everyone.

In Dayton's Allen Elementary School, values (such as fairness and industriousness) are identified in a word of the week. The word is posted on bulletin boards, appears on cafeteria placemats, and is discussed each day in every classroom. Every Friday, the entire student body and faculty gather around the flagpole to watch a skit put on by students to dramatize what the word means. The principal notes the impact of the ritual on behavior: "The whole school revolves around teaching the values represented in the word of the week."

The main problem with rules is that they are "made to be broken" because they are usually enforced by authority figures. Rituals dictate behavior in less visible and obtrusive ways. Conformity to professional values is an individual's moral responsibility, carefully monitored by the entire group. In many respects, rituals have a decided functional advantage over rules because internalized conformity becomes a shared responsibility rather than being mandated from above. For example, at Audubon Elementary School in Baton Rouge, Louisiana, a ritual exchange of information on upcoming workshops or seminars works better than rules requiring that the information be posted.[15]

Rituals are routines that have deeper norms and values embedded in them. Rituals that support collaboration, collegiality, and renewal powerfully promote school improvement.

## Ceremonies as Communication Media

As previously stated, the beginning and end of a fiscal or school year and special events should be marked by celebrations. Ceremonies provide a cultural space in which stories are told, rituals are enacted, and heroes and heroines are anointed or remembered. During these special events, there is a deeper form of communication that takes place below the surface. Celebrations join past, present, and future. While bonding people to one another and to the important values they share, celebrations provide a functional means for communication. They link myth and structure so that myth has form and structure comes alive.

Jo Ann Harrison, the principal of a new school in Broward County launched the year with an announcement: the school had been adopted by the city baseball team. In an opening session, each teacher was presented with a baseball, autographed by all the team players. As each teacher was presented the gift, the principal commented on why he or she had been selected as part of the new instructional "team."

The ending of an urban junior high school's year offers another example. During the year, an informal faculty group compiled examples of errors or failures on the part of teachers, administrators, and staff members. A closing ceremony featured these goofs in Academy Awards style. Nominations were made for the FOOGIES award (Fremont Order of Goofs in Educational Settings). The recipient received a statue of a horse's rear end. The school recognized the importance of taking risks and making mistakes on behalf of educational improvement in a humorous but ceremonial way.

Ceremonies are powerful community events that can build a shared identity, spirit, and commitment. They also communicate goals and role expectations and reinforce formal relationships and authority.

## Informal Players as Functional Roles

As noted earlier, every school creates a network of informal cultural players. These people also occupy formal roles, such as teacher, secretary, or custodian, but their unofficial duties put them in charge of traditions and symbols. Their cultural responsibilities also have functional consequences.

In a California junior high, the custodian was the school's informal priest. His intimate knowledge of the history of the school was shared with all new teachers. He was their main source of "the way we do things around here." While all new teachers receive a faculty handbook outlining formal policies, their behavior is shaped more powerfully by the informal rules passed on by the custodian. Storytellers, in spreading the lore, serve as informal coordinators. As we have already seen, stories have coordination value—if widely shared.[16] For instance, a school that has been implementing a number of new instructional and assessment approaches, regularly seeks grants, and is using site-based decision making has a staff member who knows all the stories of the school. She is available whenever visitors arrive.

Few groups really have communication problems. While the formal system may be inadequate at times, the "grapevine" usually keeps everyone up-to-date. In a southern high school, a math teacher who served as the chief gossip went so far as to have a business card made listing his title as "rumor control." As the school's eyes, ears, and voice, he ensures that everyone, including the principal, knows what everyone else is doing. Neither memos nor formal announcements over the school's public address system are as effective as he and the other message passers in the informal network.

### Memoranda as Poetry

Memoranda are often mundane and downright boring. As a result, they are disposed of before being read or scanned with little joy or attention. Really vivid memos can be more functional than dull if methodical ones in communicating important issues to different areas of groups. The "Fat Lady Sings" memo from a middle school (Exhibit 5.1) provides an excellent example of how memoranda can become more functional when they have pizzazz.

The announcements serve their intended purposes of circulating information but do so in an interesting way. The chances are good that this memo was read and attended to.

Exhibit 5.1. "The Fat Lady Sings" Memo.

*"Success is a journey, not a destination."*

---

## THE FAT LADY SINGS
### February 12, 1985

| | |
|---|---|
| I ONLY HAVE A PEN | Please bring a #2 pencil in today's faculty meeting to fill out a SACS questionnaire. |
| LOCKED OUT | Is there any reason for the lounge to be locked in the morning? Some of us come early, and we are unable to sign in. |
| BLACKOUT | Why are there no lights in the front hall on the 3rd floor? Are we on an austerity campaign? Someone falling, tripping, or hiding will ultimately cost more than light bulbs. |
| CHANGES ON THE WAY | At the volunteer faculty meeting yesterday afternoon, the following concerns were discussed: |

(1) Too many interruptions over the PA system: The PA system will normally be used only during homeroom and the LAST FIVE MINUTES of the school day. At any other time, it will be used only in cases of emergency.

(2) Conflicting information and directions given by the office: Any information/directions printed in the Fat Lady should be considered accurate and final. If the information or directions are later changed, the "buzz words" will be "Contrary to what has been said in the Fat Lady."

(3) New procedures which change the schedule of the school day: Change will always cause some frustration. Although the office will attempt to inform teachers beforehand, teachers are also responsible for suggesting ideas/opinions/concerns to the office. Teachers must trouble-shoot—just as administrators do. All of us are responsible for the policies of the school.

| | |
|---|---|
| I'LL BELIEVE IT WHEN I SEE IT | David Jackson from computer service called and said our report cards should be ready by Wednesday. Keep your fingers crossed. |
| TO THE OFFICE | Thank you from Susan, Patti, Wallace, Colette, Janet, and Nancy for not interrupting the last ten minutes of our seventh-period classes yesterday with announcements.[17] |

---

*Play as Work*

During the past two or three decades, schools have been under pressure to clarify goals, set measurable objectives, evaluate teachers and programs more systematically, and rationalize procedures. Teaching has become hard work, and time spent "on task" has become a measure of successful instruction. Play has become a marginal activity, but it is crucial to schools.[18]

Decreasing play in schools is counterproductive because play has important functional outcomes. It relieves tension, keeps people from getting so tight that they cannot work well, and brings them together. More important, play is a primary source of creativity and invention. Albert Einstein once commented that the gift of fantasy was more meaningful to him than his talent for absorbing knowledge. In order to work better, schools may have to encourage people to play more. One principal, for example, promised to eat fried worms if all the students in school read six books each over vacation (they did, and he kept his promise—although their task was certainly more pleasant than his). After successful test scores were made public, another principal spent the day on the roof accompanied by his desk, chair, and telephone.

Playfulness communicates the human acceptance of mistakes, the pleasure of success, and the importance of humor. The seriousness of schooling is actually enhanced by the use of play.

## Final Thoughts

Effective schools are those that balance structure and culture in a dynamic tension that keeps the fulcrum point on center. Principals need to encourage dramatic routine and functional drama, "porpoiseful" policy and purposeful play.

Bifocal principals understand the importance of viewing schools as productive factories and as value-shaping temples. But, more important, they understand how routine activities must reflect the culture and how rituals can also serve formal purposes. By simultaneously making routines dramatic and rituals functional, principals and other school leaders work to develop meaningful, productive schools for themselves, their staffs, and their students.

Meaning and production come together in a balanced school that is existentially buoyant and instructionally efficient, precious and proficient, beloved and focused. Symbolic and technical views, rather than remaining separate and antagonistic, combine to create a high-quality school with deep values and efficient roles.

# Chapter Six

# Getting There

Change and improvement are prominent features in educational history and a focal point of today's educational landscape. But despite huge investments in updating curricula, instruction, and other practices and patterns of schools, we see few signs that the desired dividends are yet realized. Change and improvement remain important and valued ends but extremely difficult to achieve. A case from the past illustrates some of the enduring issues. What happened in the Timber River School District nearly twenty years ago seems strangely familiar in light of current reform efforts.[1]

### Change and Improvement: A Case from the Past

The opportunity given to a select group of small rural school districts in the 1970s seemed almost too good to be true. Ten districts had been selected to be part of the federally funded Experimental Schools Program. Each district was given a sizable amount of money to reinvent schools. The program encouraged comprehensive changes instead of previous piecemeal alterations that had heretofore rarely resulted in any significant improvement.

To the superintendent of the Timber River Schools, among the chosen ten, word that the district had been awarded a $1.2 million grant was a dream come true—at least he thought so initially. The district already had been involved in a major improvement effort for several years. The additional funds would now help put the icing on the cake. At the school opening meeting, the superintendent was surprised and thrown off balance by the reaction of the faculty as he announced the major award. He had expected this obvious feather in the district's cap to be received with enthusiasm and pride. Instead of appreciative applause at the end of his remarks, however, the faculty gave the superintendent its resounding disapproval. A faculty member rose to his feet, pointed his finger at the superintendent, and shouted, "You dare to make such a decision without consulting the faculty?"

This was only the beginning of a string of surprises that ultimately undermined the hopes of the district. More rancor was to come as the district planned and carried out the proposed improvements. During the planning year, broad-based participation generated hundreds of ideas from teachers, parents, and community members about how their schools could be improved. An outside consultant was hired to help assemble the multitude of good ideas into a unified improvement plan. But not only was his final product unreadable, nearly every group that had been involved in the planning process felt that its ideas were not represented adequately in the final document. When it was presented to the representative steering committee, only two of the original eighteen members even bothered to show up.

Yet even more turmoil lay ahead. As the planned improvements began to materialize, conflicts erupted between the administrators who insisted that the plan be followed as written—"Do what we agreed"—and the teachers who reiterated that they had almost no influence in shaping the plan. They therefore did not feel bound by its contents. The internal conflicts soon spilled over into the community when a parents group raised concerns about using students as "guinea pigs." The parents formed a coalition with teachers and through a well-organized political campaign defeated the superintendent's supporters on the school board. Under pressure from his new board, the superintendent was forced to back off from many of the proposed changes.

This scenario is a familiar version of what happens frequently as districts and schools move toward site-based management, performance assessment, restructuring, or other contemporary innovations designed to improve educational productivity. Many of these are encountering forms of resistance (visible or behind the scenes) that are similar to those in Timber River. But strategies never seem to change; very little is learned from the mistakes of the past, and they are repeated again and again.

Below the surface of Timber River's commotion, unrecognized and unresolved technical and symbolic issues were causing many formidable problems. Had the administration dealt with these issues more effectively, the proposed Experimental Schools improvements might have wended their way more successfully into district educational patterns and practices. In this chapter, we will try our hand at integrating two different images of what change is all about. Very often, our knowledge about the change process partitions technical and symbolic approaches into mutually exclusive categories. Administrators' relying on one approach and neglecting others is one reason why similar versions of what happened at Timber River many years ago keep occurring. Changing the all-too-familiar scenario is going to require the bifocal vision and bimodal action of principals who move cautiously ahead after taking to heart what Machiavelli said many years ago: "It should be borne in mind that there is nothing more difficult to handle, more doubtful of success, and more dangerous to carry through than initiating changes. . . . The innovator makes enemies of all those who prospered under the old order, and only lukewarm support is forthcoming from those who would prosper under the new."[2]

## Change as a Technical Challenge

Most past reform initiatives have reflected rational-technical assumptions. From this viewpoint, the target of change is typically the structure of schools. Schools need more well-defined goals and objectives. Teachers at the local level must be given clear responsibilities and held accountable for results. Parents are to be involved in shaping purposes and making decisions through some form of site council. The process of changing itself is highly rational. Together, parents, teachers, and administrators analyze the gap between current and desired performance. From this appraisal, the school develops an improvement plan, establishes an organized process for making it operational, and designs an ongoing and systematic program of monitoring and evaluation. Many such efforts overlook the fact that change is more than just a technical challenge; it also requires cultural transitions and transformations.

## Change as Cultural Transition

Some recent attempts to change schools have assumed that the problem is symbolic and concerns values in addition to being technical. From this vantage point, the issue of change looks very different. If anything, each attempt at progress takes us a step backward. Wave after wave of reform, rather than helping, has actually caused the cultural fabric of schools to weaken and unravel. Rather than inventing new, more sophisticated forms of teaching and learning, a symbolic approach often calls for the revival of time-tested patterns and practices. It also seeks improvement through strengthening existing cultural patterns—articulating core values, encouraging ritual and ceremony to join people in a common quest, and relying heavily on symbols and stories to communicate success. By attending to cultural elements, the vitality of schools can be restored or renewed. Although these assumptions have some validity, they also miss something important. Change is not only a cultural transition. Both symbolic *and* technical considerations need constant attention and require frequent support.[3]

## Blending the Two Approaches

There is no defensible reason why these two approaches to school reform have to be mutually exclusive. Planning can incorporate vision and values into objectives. Pinpointing discrepancies between existing and desired ends can encompass rituals and traditions as well as achievement scores. As we have seen, the process of planning itself can be an important cultural ritual or ceremony as well as a problem-solving activity. As changes move from abstraction to action, training can serve both acculturation and skill-building ends. As changes are enacted, realigning formal roles and relationships can be accompanied by transition rituals helping people let go of traditional ways. These rituals can ensure that proposed changes are knitted, naturally and meaningfully, into everyday life. Evaluation efforts can collect and disseminate stories of success just as easily as computing facts and figures. Enlisting the cultural network, as well as those in positions of formal authority, can help to diminish the warfare that often occurs between guardians of the status quo and the champions of change.

Balancing these seemingly irreconcilable differences will require the attention of principals who can play the game impressively two ways—as technical problem-solvers *and* as symbolic culture-shapers. Changing a school successfully often requires three things of principals: (1) improving their technical capabilities, (2) developing or refining their symbolic sensitivities, and (3) learning when a rational event might present an opportunity to deal with symbolic issues (or vice versa).

## The Stages of Change

The process of change in schools is often broken into three overlapping stages: planning, implementation, and institutionalization. Though actually the stages take the form of a spiral rather than a linear progression, each phase presents key challenges that need to be overcome. For example, planning efforts are typically plagued by unclear and conflicting goals. Both individuals and special-interest groups generally have trouble reaching consensus on what needs to be done. The challenge of establishing a new shared direction often appears so overwhelming that conflicts and disagreements are ignored or downplayed, only to resurface in destructive ways later on.[4]

Implementation is the process of putting the plan into action. This is the critical phase where specified improvements are undercut and the status quo is reaffirmed. As plans are being carried out, several barriers often present themselves: (1) people do not have the required skills to do what is being asked of them, (2) people have emotional ties to timeworn practices that are being replaced, (3) predictability and security give way to confusion and fear, (4) needed resources such as time, materials, or energy are in shorter supply than initially predicted, and (5) prochange people begin to lock horns with the protectors of the status quo. Problems of implementation keep many of the desired improvements from becoming a regular, widely accepted part of everyday life. By keeping both the technical and symbolic challenges in clear view, it is possible to turn many of these perennial traps into exciting new possibilities. Technical approaches help to manage more effectively what is happening on the surface. Symbolic strategies help to spot and resolve cultural issues bubbling underneath the rational veneer.

## The Challenges of Planning

Technical logic advocates several steps for planning change more effectively. Planning often begins with the collection of data about existing school and student performance through surveys, academic achievement tests, and other measures. From this information, principals and the planning teams target areas that need to be improved and then identify potential strategies. These are usually spelled out in some detail in an improvement plan that includes outlines for week-to-week—even day-to-day—activities. Specific, quantifiable criteria help the school stay on course when predictable resistance exerts backward pressure.

Good technical planning involves clarifying goals and garnering support by various groups and factions within the school. Time spent in specifying and negotiating purpose, direction, problems, and ownership early helps to minimize the all-too-familiar difficulties that Timber River administrators had to wrestle with later on.

It is also important to clarify various roles and responsibilities that will be involved in implementation. Too often, people commit themselves to the plan without a sense of what it will mean for their particular roles or positions of authority. As difficulties arise, it is often the principal who is left holding the bag because responsibility for getting specific things done was never spelled out.

Good technical planning details the array of resources that will be required. It takes time for teachers and others to meet, develop new skills, and observe new programs in other schools. Money is needed to pay for training, new materials, or more staff members. Additional personnel—trainers, consultants, or clerical staffers—are often required to coach teachers, give advice, or handle the details. Unless these resource needs are identified and included in the budget, the improvement effort will quickly collapse under the added weight of new demands and responsibilities.

Even if these technical challenges are handled effectively, planning can still run into trouble if important symbolic issues are not given enough attention. As an example, who is to be on the planning team? A typical approach is to fill the planning team with innovative people who are inherently prochange. This leaves out less supportive but still powerful teachers and makes them resentful. Often, they convene their own planning group to prepare a counterattack or contemplate guerilla action. Involving more traditionally oriented people may result in a less ambitious plan, but their participation often improves the probability that the plan will become a reality. Including representatives from the school's informal cultural network, for example, helps to ensure that the planning team will not become an isolated subculture, detached from the rest of the school. Information thereby flows quickly and easily to everyone, not just to a restricted few.

The second tactical error that planners often make is to focus on the present and future without looking backward. Where we have been determines where we will head and whether the future will be rooted in or disconnected from the past. Visions that have no links with history are often ignored or resisted. As historical sleuth, the principal learns of the past and, where possible, tries to graft promising new programs onto strong old roots.

In one school, the principal and staff escorted everyone through a public presentation of the history of the school. Concerns, fears, and past problems surfaced that would make any new changes automatically suspect. Several prior improvement projects had left many festering wounds. A previous principal had started a major change effort and then left precipitately. Several new instructional programs in which teachers had significant personal investments were suddenly dropped. In previous planning efforts, furthermore, representatives of various factions had attacked others personally and unprofessionally. These injuries were attended to and discussed in the historical replay. Old wounds were dressed, and injured individuals were supported as the mending occurred. Without such healing, these past symbolic injuries could have caused continuing problems later on.

A third common tactical error is failing to infuse goals with passion and meaning. *Goals* are statements of desired end points, usually specified in quantifiable terms. A *vision* is a mental image of a better and more hopeful future. Visions engage people's hearts as well as their heads—especially when widely shared. Because visions are ephemeral, they are generally expressed in mottoes, phrases, or symbols that arouse passion as well as communicate direction and purpose.

Good planning also serves as a meaningful ritual that draws people together emotionally and spiritually. Values and hopes are connected to objectives. The planning ritual provides the opportunity to break down the isolation and individualism of teaching through collaborative discussion, collegial sharing, and reflection practice. All can be powerful cultural experiences.

A fourth tactical symbolic error of planning teams is to overlook spirit as a needed resource in making plans operational. Human spirit is an essential part of any organization. It is an essential source of energy and makes a vital contribution to top performance. Good planning addresses how to create a reservoir of human spirit that can encourage changes. Otherwise, ample time, money, materials, and other tangible resources will be insufficient. Planning should anticipate how people's hopes and spirit will be maintained and enhanced as plans become a part of everyday practice.

### The Challenges of Implementation

Plans never reach goals or achieve dreams if they are not implemented. Implementation, once seen as simply following the defined action steps of the plan, is in fact a complicated and demanding mix of cultural transition and technical activity. Studies of educational reform provide multiple examples of how even the best-laid plans fall apart when they encounter the realities of complex human organizations.[5] Although many of the problems of making plans operational can be foreseen and addressed by the planning team, others become obvious only when action is taken. It is all too easy to get caught up in the excitement of change in the abstract and to forget that people rarely relish the reality of changing. They are for change as long as they do not have to do anything differently themselves.

There are several technical issues that emerge quickly in the operational phase of improvement.[6] Each places added demands on a principal's already strained capabilities. First, coordination issues intensify. Under stable conditions, responsibilities can often be synchronized through administrative decisions or school policy. However, changes typically create so much ambiguity and added complexity that coordination among various groups has to be done face to face and on the fly. More time is thereby needed to get things done. The amount of time necessary often exceeds resource forecasts made during early stages of the planning process. Principals find it necessary to develop multiple coordination options and usually have to find new ways to help staff members know what they are supposed to do, how their efforts relate to others, and who is in charge of what. This is especially true when improvement is a collaborative process. Planning never stops with the formulation of a plan. It has to be evolutionary as the process unfolds.

Second, new problems always surface that often fall beyond principals' customary analytic repertoire. How do they reassure parents about new instructional approaches when, despite initial inservice training, many teachers themselves still have their doubts? How do they find time to deal with anticipated confusion when everyone is already overloaded? How can principals provide answers when they themselves are unclear about exactly what to do or what the outcomes will be? Having a representative steering committee or council that can sort through the issues and communicate with staff and the public expands available analytic capabilities. Within such groups, the principal's role often shifts from the individual analyst who provides the answers to the facilitator of a collective identification of underlying problems and solutions.

Third, initiatives to improve educational practices generate new pressures on the boundaries among insiders and important external constituencies. At the first hint that something different is afoot, parents, the media, interested citizens, and other professionals want to know exactly what is going on. Business as usual rarely generates much outside interest; innovation stimulates curiosity and concern. Parents worry about experimentation; the media are often after a good story; and the local citizenry wants assurance that new programs are not creating more costs that will eventually mean higher taxes. And the school districts next door are curious because of their own need to keep up with what is currently in fashion. Visitors from other school systems can take up considerable time and energy in their efforts to understand and imitate promising new practices.

Principals have to figure out how to handle the extra activity at the boundary. Otherwise, already overtaxed human resources will be overwhelmed with the flood of complaints, questions, and requests for additional information. Moreover, change often attracts newcomers—prospective staff members looking for an exciting challenge—at the same time that it encourages old-timers who are set in their ways to seek early retirement. Issues surrounding who comes and who stays add even more burdens to the principal's gatekeeping role. Providing access while controlling the flow of people entering and leaving requires constant attention.

Fourth, anytime something unusual occurs, people want information, firsthand knowledge about what it means to them and to those they care about. Part of this communication challenge comes from outside the school as various groups want to be kept up to date. Newsletters, informal coffees, and other strategies help to keep people posted. In one school, the principal sends a letter to parents and other interested citizens at the end of each school year describing improvement efforts and discussing what worked and what needs to be done differently in the coming year.

Internally, the professionals responsible for making the changes also require current information. They need access to professionals who work outside the school, information about research and best practice, and the chance to reflect on the ideas. The principal's role as disseminator often requires an active link with local and national reform groups, regional experts, and local schools of education to ensure that teachers and others have the latest information about what is happening elsewhere. This practice helps to separate generic problems from local issues and to pinpoint what needs to be done to fine-tune things within a school. Here again, the principal's position in the information network is often a critical factor in how well plans are carried out. Principals become gatherers and disseminators of critical information, ideas, and sources of ideas.

Fifth, supervision plays a key role in determining how long new skills and approaches persist after an initial training. Too often, training is a "one shot" effort whose effects dissipate quickly in the press of everyday detail, problems, and pressure to change. Supportive supervision provides helpful feedback to reinforce and refine newly acquired skills. Since the principal continues to engage in daily problem solving, new forms of supervision can be extremely helpful as improvement plans become operational. Peer coaching (giving experienced teachers informal supervisional responsibilities) or inviting well-respected retirees to assist can be valuable approaches to supervision. Redirecting human resources at the district office from compliance to support roles is another option. The Aurora School District in Colorado has created a cadre of facilitators, volunteers from both certified and classified staff members who are available to be called on to provide assistance in a broad range of areas related to instructional and organizational improvement efforts.

Finally, change inherently breeds conflict within levels, between levels, and among various interest groups, individuals, and departments. Some of these support the changes; others are just as determined in their defense of the status quo. Conflict can quickly become warfare unless mechanisms are developed to manage disputes and negotiate compromises among the competing interests. Procedures for regulating disputes can be specified and agreed upon during the planning phase. In some schools, the governing council provides a forum where disagreements are aired and negotiated before hostilities become increasingly bitter or fester underground. One thoughtful principal, tired of dealing with all the disputes herself, created a special peace-making room where disagreements would be taken. Special rules governed behavior in the room. Well-trained facilitators often served as mediators.

But even with procedures in place to manage conflict, it is often the principal who is called upon to adjudicate, negotiate, and build agreements among varied interest groups and staff members. Rather than treating conflict as negative, the principal as jurist sees it as a source of energy and a chance to work through existing differences. Through open arenas or behind-the-scenes mediation, disagreements are dealt with in a fair and open manner.

### The Deeper Symbolic Challenges of Implementing Change

Successful implementation is only partially ensured by confronting and managing the technical problems that crop up as planned improvements are launched and integrated into school routines. Most changes require transformation in deeper patterns of people's thoughts, feelings, and beliefs. Traditional mindsets need to be revised and the symbolic tapestry of the school needs to be rewoven to provide cultural support for new ways of thinking and acting. Successful transformation requires letting go of traditional patterns, entering into a temporary void or open space, and eventually latching onto the new improved patterns, practices, and beliefs. For anyone, this process is frightening, disorienting, and upsetting. Helping a school through a process that avoids people holding tightly onto old ways or plunging recklessly and prematurely into innovative practices taxes a principal's symbolic talents to the limit.

The foundation for the successful launch of new programs is constructed during the planning phase as the principal becomes a historian to uncover the school's past experience with change and an anthropological detective to identify current players in the informal network of the school. In trying to navigate an open space where neither old or new ways dominate, wise principals stay in touch with the school's unofficial priests or priestesses. As keepers of the tradition, these individuals can create powerful barriers to block progress or to support change. Consulted frequently and respected for what they can offer, these people can help to weave the spirit of the past into new innovative traditions.

As we noted earlier, the principal's official role of communicator can be amplified substantially by connections with unofficial gossips and storytellers. In one school, the gossip was "semiofficially" given a reduced load with more time to confirm, deny, check out, or spread the latest word about the progress of proposed changes. Oregon's Beaverton School District provides time each year for its storytellers to highlight the "pits and berries" of the preceding year. Annually, cultural support is built for the continual changes under way in district schools.

As changes are initiated, the importance of the principal's symbolic role in representing desired values and practices increases substantially. In times of transition, people look to the principal for signs of how things are going and where they are headed. They want an anchor point for assurance that everything is going to be all right. It is helpful when the principals and other school leaders demonstrate values of experimentation, risk taking, courage, and collaboration. As an example, the principal of a school trying a new approach to assessing students is first in line to test its reliability and the alternative measures that have been developed. She herself demonstrates a willingness to give it a try and the bravery to make her trials and errors visible to everyone.

As innovations move along, principals working with others help to support the changes. They anoint emerging new heroes and heroines (those whose risk taking, hard work, and collegial improvement efforts exemplify the best). They encourage symbols to help reinforce core values and assumptions of emerging new ways and traditions. These cultural elements assist in uniting diverse subcultures of students, staff members, parents, and community into a shared enterprise so that everyone can identify with and feel inspired by the new directions.

A sense of shared endeavor can be accomplished through many specific actions:

- Establishing end-of-year traditions for celebrating the success of programs (and properly burying those that have died).
- Bestowing rewards and recognition on those who have weathered the hurricanes of change (for example, one principal gives the "combat award" each year to the teacher who has taken on the most innovative challenges and survived the "battles").
- Distributing symbols of the process—logos, notebooks for the task forces, and rooms designated for the improvement team to meet, confer, and post notices.
- Recognizing the contributions and support of parents in awards ceremonies at school.

As a poet, the principal can articulate the inspiring, abstract hopes and dreams of the change effort through metaphors, stories, and prose. This is not an easy task when many things are in transition. Implementing changes often makes a school a virtual Tower of Babel. Principals struggle to discover a new shared language that is positive and uplifting. School traditions sometimes unconsciously foster language that demeans students, deflates motivation, and demoralizes anyone who challenges the status quo. As a counterforce to these negative cultural patterns, principals can be lucid and eloquent in communicating the motivating new words and messages that can draw the school community together. For example, the principal of "Williamson Elementary School" constantly talks about how "all children can learn." She speaks eloquently of the collegiality and collaboration of the staff and extols its devotion to the improvement of instruction for all the students.[7]

While not always in iambic pentameter or presented with the timbre of a Shakespearian actor, principals' language can play a powerful role in articulating what the school might become and communicating the hope that it can get there.

School dramas intensify as people in changing circumstances take on new roles and struggle with unfamiliar scripts. It is important that these everyday dramas are reenacted on stage in front of an audience. Principals can play an active part in orchestrating theater that helps people deal with the travails of transition and learning new responsibilities. In one school, for example, the theater features the principal as a "referee" while teachers engage in mock battle over whether the school should be completely restructured into interdisciplinary teams. The battleground is a theater, and theater has become an important part of the change process. Good theater needs a director to keep the discussion and dialogue in bounds and make sure the actors stay in character. Sometimes the principal provides such direction. At other times, he or she assumes whatever roles (starring or supporting) are necessary to keep the drama (and at times comedy) of change alive and in full view.

Change inevitably creates stress, loss, and pain. As previously mentioned, new and previously unresolved conflicts need to be settled as the process of implementing new programs moves along.

There are many who can help heal these unavoidable disputes, but
the principal often plays a central role.

In one school, the principal convenes her teachers and staff
each year on the final day. The event is designed as a wake or
funeral in which retiring teachers, old programs, and other losses
are recognized and their leaving is officially mourned. When the
new year begins, the faculty returns to find pictures and memorabilia of departed people and programs hung on the wall of the
teachers' lounge. The new year is then officially launched from a
perspective of rich heritage and historical legacy.

As people let go of old traditions and practices, they need
something to replace them. They need an inspiring image of what
the future might become and a shared hope that it will eventually
materialize. A vision, however primitive, pulls staff members, students, parents, and others under the same symbolic banner even
while everything is in flux. Without shared vision or hope, improvement efforts bog down in administrative trivia and petty bick-
ering and may eventually founder on the reefs of hidden problems
or open resistance. Though principals are not always prophets, they
can craft an embryonic vision from the subconscious wishes and
dreams deeply embedded in the school community.

### The Hopes for Institutionalization

The final stage of the change process is institutionalization. This
occurs when the new structures, roles, norms, values, and beliefs
have become an organic part of everyday living, working, and feeling in the school. It happens when routines are rituals and rituals
become routine. A new curriculum or instructional activity has become so much a part of the formal structure *and* of the deeper
foundations of the culture that it is now accepted as "the way we
do things around here." At this stage, the ongoing and regular
features of the roles, budgets, and schedules provide the technical
basis and the school culture, with its rituals, traditions, and ceremonies, has knitted the new into the evolving social fabric.[8]

Here the blended roles of the principal support the program
or activity by providing effective managerial support and sensitive
symbolic reinforcement. The deepest and most enduring way that

programs and practices become embedded in schools is by being institutionalized into both the formal and the social structure of the school.

Across the various phases of change, school principals can play a vital role if they can read and respond to both technical and symbolic challenges. Very often, rational responses can also serve symbolic ends, and vice versa. Hank Cotton, a principal we introduced in Chapter Five, demonstrates how this approach can work.

### Changing Cherry Creek High School

When Hank Cotton assumed the principalship of Cherry Creek High School, he was faced with a formidable challenge.[9] The school, located in an affluent Denver suburb, was like many high schools of the 1970s. In the innovative spirit of the times, Cherry Creek had liberalized its authority structure, relaxed formal expectations, increased instructional options for students, and become an "open campus" school.

The results of the schoolwide restructuring had not been good. Courses proliferated. In-class attendance declined—to below 80 percent during some class periods. Teachers "canceled" classes whenever they wished. Sanctions for cutting either class or school were not regularly reinforced. Community concerns about academic achievement and student drug use intensified. Five principals in six years had tried to do something about the situation. Most left, according to the teachers, without "really unpacking their bags."

Many of Cotton's initial actions displayed an obvious structural-technical overlay. He immediately set two primary goals: increasing student responsibility and improving academic performance. His first objective was to deal with excessive absenteeism, an obvious barrier to learning. He instituted new attendance policies requiring students—and teachers—to meet their scheduled classes. At first, more than 235 students were suspended for infractions of the policy, creating an uproar from parents. Cotton's new parking rule, prohibiting cars on school lawns, also raised a furor when a son of a school board member was the first to have his car towed for violating the policy.

Cotton's next series of policy changes focused on the instructional practices at Cherry Creek. He established a new, demanding system of evaluating teachers to give them feedback on their classroom performance. He formally requested the social studies department to redesign its curriculum, consolidating seventy electives into a more focused, integrated set of offerings. He changed the method of selecting department chairs; he himself assumed authority for appointing the chairs rather than having them elected by teachers in the departments. All of these changes created intense conflict, which he met head on in his role as jurist. Relying heavily on technical assumptions, Cotton sought to restructure the school, to restore order and create a more predictable, focused, goal-directed enterprise.

Many of Cotton's structural moves had implicit symbolic undertones. Attendance and teacher evaluation policies, for example, signaled a renewed emphasis on the values of teaching and learning. Other structural changes also reinforced the new commitment to teaching and learning as core cultural values. Cotton did away with teacher "administrivia," giving the responsibility for hall duty, cafeteria duty, study hall supervision, and the checking of permission passes to noncertificated personnel. He publicly rewarded teachers and administrators who demonstrated the values of excellence, improvement, and collegiality. He found resources for top teachers to attend conferences, purchase materials for special projects, and receive summer pay for working collegially with other teachers to improve instruction. He gave the student government additional authority, office space, and regular access to the principal. He never turned down an opportunity to meet with any group to communicate the hopes and dreams that he had for Cherry Creek High School. During these frequently emotionally charged events, he gave people a chance to ventilate and move on. He realized that many of his changes represented losses for other people, even though their attachments had fastened onto questionable educational values. He was highly visible at concerts, athletic contests, honor society banquets, and other important ceremonies. Although his first two years were full of turmoil, the changes began to jell, and a more positive culture started to evolve.

Cotton's symbolic sense was just as strong as his technical skills. Before taking the position, he had acquainted himself with the early history of Cherry Creek High. Rather than imposing his values on the school, he sought to remind students, teachers, and parents that student learning was a key value in the original mission of the school. He himself showed high standards of performance and professionalism and made it a point to attend seminars and executive development programs to improve his own work. He regularly carried with him novels and history books and quoted these works in his memos and speeches.

Cotton was a veritable library of stories about individuals who exemplified the emerging values and traditions. In talking with newcomers, outsiders, or the media, he would often start the conversation with several stories of success at the school. Cotton made extensive use of ceremonies, rituals, traditions, and symbols to reinforce the new priorities. He deliberately changed his "uniform" for important schoolwide ceremonies; he brought a dark suit to change into for honors ceremonies or evening award events. He had bumper stickers printed that stated "Let the Tradition Continue" and "The Legend Lives On." He referred to success as part of a tradition: "We traditionally send many students East." An avid jogger, he would not run without the school "Bruin" on his exercise shoes. When the district office developed a poster, "Onward to Excellence," Cotton made one for the school, "Beyond Excellence to Greatness," which was displayed prominently in his office.

Finally, Cotton worked diligently to find new faculty members who held the values he was trying to inculcate. The selection procedures were so rigorous that new teachers in their first year frequently worried about whether they were measuring up to the high standards. Teachers committed to the old regime who could not accept the changes that Cotton was making were encouraged to accept positions elsewhere. All of Cotton's symbolic flourishes focused attention on learning as a central value and student achievement as a top-priority goal. Over time, teachers, department chairs, and students developed collaborative efforts to maintain the values and traditions of quality in the school. By creating a culture emphasizing collegiality, professionalism, and high standards, he was able implicitly to shape coordination, supervision, and other aspects of formal structure. Although he initiated these changes, the culture of the staff maintained it as well. Shared mores, rather than explicit rules and policies, soon began to govern everyday behavior in the school. Stories of uncommon exploits flooded the school communication network, displacing negative rumors that had dominated for years.

Hank Cotton's ambidextrous approach to educational change was one of the key factors in the turnaround at Cherry Creek. He relied on both policies and symbols to get the job done. He realized that technical activity influences cultural values and that stories and policies are mutually reinforcing. Cotton demonstrates that paradoxical roles can be fused in unusual combinations to make changes that are simultaneously sensible and meaningful. He assumed seemingly contradictory roles of a healing jurist, symbolic supervisor, poetic-information disseminator, and ritualistic coordinator. In the process, he helped Cherry Creek High surmount the technical and symbolic challenges of change.

# Chapter Seven

# Epilogue

Today's pressures on the principalship show no signs of decreasing in their intensity. Future challenges include encouraging dispersed yet centered leadership, creating a cohesive community out of increasingly diverse populations, being responsible without being in charge, changing rapidly in response to social needs without leaving people behind, building trust and confidence in an openly cynical society, and caring for people while challenging them to grow. Together, these challenges will continue to fill every principal's day with problems to solve, puzzles to unravel, and paradoxes to manage or endure.

In order to survive and thrive in these increasingly complex, unpredictable situations, principals will need cognitive templates and action repertoires that enable them to respond effectively to both technical and symbolic issues. Technical problems require the analytic, rational problem-solving capabilities of a well-organized manager. Symbolic dilemmas require the sensitive, expressive touch of an artistic and passionate leader. Tomorrow's principal in our view will be asked to be a combination of both—or to spot and empower others who can provide the managerial efficiency or the leadership energy and vision that the principal cannot. Whichever route a principal takes, in the educational world of the future, it will be increasingly difficult to partition management and leadership into mutually exclusive categories. All organizations, including schools, need a blend of passion and order, faith and results, meaning and measurement.

How will principals develop the diverse talent and understanding that more balanced administrative approaches demand? Many of these abilities will come from experience and reflective conversations with colleagues. There is little reason to believe that traditional preparation programs, housed in universities, will help bridge technical and symbolic orientations. At their best, universities provide a rational-technical background for assuming a principalship. Almost none balance this important technical foundation with exposure to the expressive world of myth, story, theater, ritual, ceremony, humor, music, or play. Unless this existing imbalance shifts in the foreseeable future, principals will have to augment their preparation on their own, in principal centers or in programs (such as the California School Leaders Academy) that have widened their scope to include symbolism and culture as central topics.

On their own and with their colleagues, we think that principals can develop or rediscover the symbolic side of their work. We have intended this book to develop in principals and other school leaders a yen for reading literature, poetry, or philosophy; watching movies; going to the theater; listening to music; and weaving artistic forms into their jobs. Without a deep understanding of the expressive side of the human equation, principals will be less able to respond to what goes on beneath the rational surface of situations or learn fully the important lessons that experience can teach.

In closing, the hidden hazards of managing and leading educational organizations will probably never disappear. The work of principals may never again become the simple role of the past. But by discovering, inventing, and creating new combinations of technical and symbolic ways of thinking and taking action, we are convinced that the future responsibilities of principals can be even more exciting, playful, and productive than they are today. As a consequence, the schools of our nation will again produce the results and maintain the faith that society legitimately expects.

# Notes

### Preface

1.  A fascinating historical view of school principals is found in Lynn G. Beck and Joseph Murphy, *Understanding the Principalship: Metaphorical Themes, 1920s–1990s* (New York: Teachers College Press, 1993).
2.  Much of the research on principals has looked at the nature of their work, with special attention to managerial tasks and instructional leadership. See Harry Wolcott, *The Man in the Principal's Office* (Troy, Mo.: Holt, Rinehart & Winston, 1973); Kent D. Peterson, "The Principal's Tasks," *The Administrator's Notebook*, 1978, *26*, 1–4; Philip Hallinger and Joseph Murphy, "Assessing the Instructional Management Behavior of Principals," *Elementary School Journal*, 1985, *85*, 217–247; and W. J. Martin and D. J. Willower, "The Managerial Behavior of High School Principals," *Educational Administration Quarterly*, 1981, *17*(1), 69–89.
3.  Institutes at places like Harvard and Vanderbilt often provide a rare opportunity for practitioners to network, reflect, and share.
4.  Lee G. Bolman and Terrence E. Deal, "Leading and Manag-

ing: Effects of Context, Culture, and Gender," *Educational Administration Quarterly,* 1992, *28*(3), 314–329.

5. A number of authors have noted the possible dualities (especially technical and symbolic ones) of managers' work. These dualities were noted in Richard L. Daft, "Symbols in Organizations: A Dual Content Framework for Analysis," in L. R. Pondy and P. Frost (eds.), *Organizational Symbolism: Monographs in Organizational Behavior and Industrial Relations* (Greenwich, Conn.: JAI Press, 1983). Also see Bruce Wilson and William A. Firestone, "The Principal and Instruction: Combining Bureaucratic and Cultural Linkages," *Educational Leadership,* 1987, *45*(1), 18–24. They note the bureaucratic and cultural linkages that principals forge in their work. Also see Ulrich C. Reitzug and Jennifer Esler Reeves, " 'Miss Lincoln Doesn't Teach Here': A Descriptive Narrative and Conceptual Analysis of a Principal's Symbolic Leadership Behavior," *Educational Administration Quarterly,* 1992, *28*(2), 185–219; Ridge E. Kelley and Paul Bredeson, "Measures of Meaning in a Public and in a Parochial School: Principals as Symbol Managers," *Journal of Educational Administration,* 1991, *29*(3), 6–22; and Terrence E. Deal and Kent D. Peterson, *Technical and Expressive Aspects of School Improvement,* paper presented at the annual conference of the International Congress of School Effectiveness and Improvement, Cardiff, Wales, 1991.

## Chapter One: Introduction: A Fence That Divides

1. Dr. Lydia Mareno and Leo are pseudonyms.
2. Excerpts of this conversation come from Linda Martinez, *Principal as Artist: A Model for Transforming a School Community,* unpublished doctoral dissertation, George Peabody College for Teachers of Vanderbilt University.
3. For a classic view, see James Thompson, *Organizations in Action* (New York: McGraw-Hill, 1967).
4. Max Weber, *The Theory of Social and Economic Organization* (New York: Oxford University Press, 1947).
5. Lee G. Bolman and Terrence E. Deal, *Modern Approaches to*

*Understanding and Managing Organizations.* (San Francisco: Jossey-Bass, 1984).

6. Raymond E. Callahan, *Education and the Cult of Efficiency* (Chicago: University of Chicago Press, 1962), provides a historical look at this orientation. Arthur Wise, *Legislated Learning: The Bureaucratization of the American Classroom* (Berkeley: University of California Press, 1979), notes the more contemporary features of this approach and some of its pitfalls.

7. Wise, *Legislated Learning.*

8. See the studies by J. T. Kmetz and Don J. Willower, "Elementary School Principals' Work Behavior," *Educational Administration Quarterly,* 1982, *18*(4), 1–29, and Kent D. Peterson, "Making Sense of Principals' Work," *The Australian Administrator,* 1982, *3*(3), 1–4.

9. Weber, *The Theory of Social and Economic Organization.*

10. The symbolic side of organizations has a long history of research. See Phillip Selznick, *Leadership and Administration* (New York: HarperCollins, 1957), who notes how organizations become institutions. Burton Clark, in "The Organizational Saga in Higher Education," *Administrative Science Quarterly,* 1972, *17*,(2), 178–184, describes the sagas and myths of organizations. Also see Terrence E. Deal and Allan Kennedy, *Corporate Cultures: The Rites and Rituals of Corporate Life* (Reading, Mass.: Addison-Wesley, 1982).

11. The work of Michael Fullan with Suzanne Stiegelbauer, *The New Meaning of Educational Change* (New York: Teachers College Press, Columbia University, 1991), provides a comprehensive look at the change process. They note the importance of culture, also described in the work of Stewart Purkey and Marshall Smith, "Effective Schools: A Review," *Elementary School Journal,* 1983, *83*, 427–452.

12. See Deal and Kennedy, *Corporate Cultures,* and Terrence E. Deal and Kent D. Peterson, *The Principal's Role in Shaping Culture* (Washington, D.C.: Department of Education, Office of Educational Research and Improvement, 1990).

13. M. T. Parker, *Images of Leadership in Broward County, Florida: Case Studies of Two Elementary School Principals,* study

undertaken for the National Center for Educational Leadership, Harvard University, 1992.

14.  Willard Waller, *The Sociology of Teaching* (New York: Wiley, 1932).

15.  Parker, *Images of Leadership in Broward County, Florida: Case Studies of Two Elementary School Principals.*

### Chapter Two: The Technician and the Artist

1.  Though it is not possible to provide an exhaustive review of the literature on the work of managers, leaders, or (specifically) school principals, here are a few of the key studies and books that might be of interest to the reader. These, of course, represent only a small part of the large body of work on school principals and their organizations: schools.

Research on the nature of managerial work, leadership, and organizations spans many decades and has occupied hundreds of scholars. See T. W. Arnold, *The Folklore of Capitalism* (New Haven, Conn.: Yale University Press, 1937); Chester Barnard, *The Functions of the Executive* (Cambridge, Mass.: Harvard University Press, 1938); and Herbert Simon, *Administrative Behavior* (New York: Free Press, 1945).

Later researchers have looked more closely at the actual tasks of managers. See Leonard R. Sayles, *Managerial Behavior: Administration in Complex Organizations* (New York: McGraw-Hill, 1964), and Henry Mintzberg, *The Nature of Managerial Work* (New York: HarperCollins, 1973). These studies provide an important foundation for understanding the technical features of these roles.

Still later, others began studying and writing about the work of school principals (see A. Lorri Manasse, "Improving Conditions for Principal Effectiveness: Policy Implications of Research," *The Elementary School Journal*, 1985, *80*, 439–463, and S. T. Bossert, D. C. Dwyer, B. Rowan, and G. V. Lee, "The Instructional Management Role of the Principal," *Educational Administration Quarterly*, 1982, *18*,(3), 34–64, for excellent reviews of these studies). The classic study of urban principals by V. C. Morris, L. Crowson, C. Porter-Gehrie, and

E. Hurwitz, Jr., *Principals in Action: The Reality of Managing Schools* (Columbus, Ohio: Merrill, 1984), also expanded what we know about the daily tasks of these administrators.

Investigations into the complexities of principals' work have added much to our knowledge. See Roland S. Barth, *Improving Schools from Within: Teachers, Parents, and Principals Can Make the Difference* (San Francisco: Jossey-Bass, 1990); A. Blumberg and W. Greenfield, *The Effective Principal: Perspectives on School Leadership* (Needham Heights, Mass.: Allyn & Bacon, 1986); W. L. Boyd and R. L. Crowson, "The Changing Conception and Practice of Public School Administration," *Review of Research in Education,* 1982, *9,* 311–373; and Dan C. Lortie, Gary Crow, and Sandra Prolman, *The Elementary School Principal in Suburbia: An Occupational and Organizational Study,* final report to National Institute of Education, U.S. Department of Education, May 1983.

2. Early work on the symbolic nature of organizations and managers by Clark, "The Organizational Saga in Higher Education," and Selznick, *Leadership and Administration,* lead the way to understanding the ways that norms, values, and beliefs shape action. More recently, our appreciation of the nature of organizational culture has been expanded by the work of Deal and Kennedy in *Corporate Cultures* and Edgar Schein in *Organizational Culture and Leadership* (San Francisco: Jossey-Bass, 1985). See also Jeffrey Pfeffer, "Management as Symbolic Action: The Creation and Maintenance of Organizational Paradigms," in L. L. Cummings and B. M. Staw (eds.), *Research in Organizational Behavior* (Greenwich, Conn.: JAI Press, 1981), and Marshall Sashkin and Herbert J. Walberg, *Educational Leadership and School Culture* (Berkeley, Calif.: McCutchan, 1993).

3. Reitzug and Reeves, "Miss Lincoln Doesn't Teach Here."

4. Charles Clancy is a composite.

5. A variety of writers have taken up the challenge of attempting to define the roles of principals and other administrators. See Mintzberg, *The Nature of Managerial Work;* Sayles, *Managerial Behavior;* Blumberg and Greenfield, *The Effective Prin-*

*cipal*; and E. B. Goldring and S. Rallis, *Principals of Dynamic Schools* (Newbury Park, Calif.: Corwin Press, 1993).

6. See K. S. Louis and M. B. Miles, *Improving the Urban High School: What Works and Why* (New York: Teachers College Press, Columbia University, 1990), for one of the best discussions of planning, especially evolutionary planning.

7. Resources are especially important in school improvement efforts. See H. D. Corbett, J. A. Dawson, and William A. Firestone, *School Context and School Change: Implications for Effective Planning* (New York: Teachers College Press, Columbia University, 1984), for a discussion.

8. One of the clearest commentaries on coordination and these features comes from Thompson, *Organizations in Action*.

9. Carl D. Glickman, *Supervision of Instruction: A Developmental Approach* (Needham Heights, Mass.: Allyn & Bacon, 1990). "Supervision Reappraised," *Update*, 1993, *35*(6), 1–4, describes some current debates about this topic.

10. While communication has always been an important part of managerial work, Mintzberg's study *The Nature of Managerial Work* illustrates the complexity and importance of this role.

11. Although there is some research on the problem-solving aspects of managers' work, its focus on solving conflicts is less evident. Mintzberg and Sayles provide useful descriptions of this responsibility.

12. The relations between schools and community have been part of the literature on school principals for decades. Some research on organizations and their environments (see Thompson, *Organizations in Action*) notes specific ways that administrators act as buffers and links with external publics and groups. In the education literature, Goldring and Rallis (*Principals of Dynamic Schools*) have particular insight into these linking functions.

13. The central role of analysis in management is implicit in much of the work of Sayles (*Leadership*) and Mintzberg (*The Nature of Managerial Work*). More recently, work on instructional leadership and school change also suggests features of

analysis. See Fullan, *The New Meaning of Educational Change.*

14. Mr. Sage is a pseudonym.

15. Reitzug and Reeves, "Miss Lincoln Doesn't Teach Here," pp. 195–196.

16. Reitzug and Reeves, "Miss Lincoln Doesn't Teach Here," p. 201.

17. Reitzug and Reeves, "Miss Lincoln Doesn't Teach Here," p. 196.

18. Reitzug and Reeves, "Miss Lincoln Doesn't Teach Here," p. 201.

19. Reitzug and Reeves, "Miss Lincoln Doesn't Teach Here," p. 202.

20. Reitzug and Reeves, "Miss Lincoln Doesn't Teach Here," p. 198.

21. Reitzug and Reeves, "Miss Lincoln Doesn't Teach Here," pp. 198–202.

22. Kidder, *Among Schoolchildren.*

23. Reitzug and Reeves, "Miss Lincoln Doesn't Teach Here," pp. 200–201.

24. Reitzug and Reeves, "Miss Lincoln Doesn't Teach Here," p. 203.

25. Reitzug and Reeves, "Miss Lincoln Doesn't Teach Here," p. 203.

26. In *The Principal's Role in Shaping Culture,* Deal and Peterson describe the roles of symbol, potter, poet, actor, and healer.

27. Knowing the history of an organization is important in any setting. This role is suggested in *The Principal's Role in Shaping Culture.*

28. These roles were first described in Deal and Kennedy, *Corporate Cultures,* then applied to schools in Deal and Peterson, *The Principal's Role in Shaping Culture.*

29. The work on the importance of vision is widespread. See Warren Bennis and Burt Nanus, *Leaders: The Strategies for Taking Charge* (New York: HarperCollins, 1985); Kent D. Peterson, "Vision and Problem Finding in Principals' Work: Values and Cognition in Administration," *Peabody Journal of Education,* 1985, *63,* 88–106; and others.

30.   Deal and Peterson, *The Principal's Role in Shaping Culture*,
      pp. 18–19.

31.   Deal and Peterson, *The Principal's Role in Shaping Culture*,
      pp. 20–23.

32.   Deal and Peterson, *The Principal's Role in Shaping Culture*,
      pp. 23–25.

33.   Deal and Peterson, *The Principal's Role in Shaping Culture*,
      p. 24.

34.   Deal and Peterson, *The Principal's Role in Shaping Culture*,
      pp. 25–27.

35.   Deal and Peterson, *The Principal's Role in Shaping Culture*,
      pp. 27–28.

36.   Deal and Peterson, *The Principal's Role in Shaping Culture*,
      pp. 28–29.

### Chapter Three: The Bifocal Principal

1.   Nancy Foy, *The Yin and Yang of Organization* (New York:
     Morrow, 1980), p. 32.

2.   The idea that managers' work serves multiple functions has
     been suggested by a number of writers. Some have identified
     the technical, managerial side of principals, and others have
     talked about the symbolic side. A few have taken a look at the
     dual roles, sometimes with perspectives different from our
     own. Simon notes in *Administrative Behavior* that all deci-
     sions have a "fact" and a "value" component to them. Later,
     others more explicitly looked at the dual nature of adminis-
     trators' responsibilities. For example, Daft in "Symbols in Or-
     ganizations" describes managerial jobs as having a dual
     content, with some having more "instrumental" aspects than
     "expressive" purposes or contents. A similar argument by
     Wilson and Firestone focuses on the dual roles of principals,
     one bureaucratic (or technical) and the other cultural (or sym-
     bolic). Several observational studies of principals' work also
     note that principals engage in symbolic work during their
     daily activities. See Reitzug and Reeves, "Miss Lincoln
     Doesn't Work Here"; Deal and Peterson, *The Principal's Role
     in Shaping Culture*; Kelley and Bredeson, "Measures of Mean-

ing"; Gretchen Rossman, Dickson Corbett, and William A. Firestone, *Change and Effectiveness in Schools: A Cultural Perspective*; and others.

3.  Robert Pirsig, *Zen and the Art of Motorcycle Maintenance: An Inquiry into Values* (New York: Bantam Books, 1984), p. 288.

4.  *Webster's New Collegiate Dictionary* (Springfield, Mass.: Merriam, 1974), p. 830.

5.  Paul Houston, "Zen and the Art of School Management," *Executive Educator*, 1990, *12*(10), p. 22.

6.  Alan Watts, *Tao: The Watercourse Way* (New York: Pantheon Books, 1975), p. 76.

7.  There are many good books on the Taoist world view. See Bob Messing, *The Tao of Management: An Age-Old Study for Modern Managers* (New York: Bantam Books, 1992).

8.  Watts, *Tao: The Watercourse Way*, p. 21.

9.  Patricia B. Bower, *Living the Leadership Paradox: The Pivotal Points of Leaders' Signals and Signaling*, unpublished doctoral dissertation, George Peabody College for Teachers of Vanderbilt University, 1989.

10.  Bower, *Living the Leadership Paradox.*

11.  Bower, *Living the Leadership Paradox.*

12.  Arthur Koestler, *The Lotus and the Robot* (New York: Macmillan, 1961), p. 235.

13.  Joseph Campbell, *Myths to Live By* (New York: Bantam Books, 1972), p. 266.

14.  Bower, *Living the Leadership Paradox.*

15.  Bower, *Living the Leadership Paradox*, p. 158.

16.  Bower, *Living the Leadership Paradox*, p. 158.

17.  Bower, *Living the Leadership Paradox*, p. 156.

18.  Bower, *Living the Leadership Paradox*, p. 185–187.

19.  Bower, *Living the Leadership Paradox*, p. 160.

20.  Bower, *Living the Leadership Paradox*, p. 162.

21.  Bower, *Living the Leadership Paradox*, p. 188.

22.  Bower, *Living the Leadership Paradox*, p. 166.

23.  Bower, *Living the Leadership Paradox*, p. 183.

24.  Bower, *Living the Leadership Paradox*, p. 170.

25.  Bower, *Living the Leadership Paradox*, p. 173.

26.  Bower, *Living the Leadership Paradox*, p. 175.

27.  Bower, *Living the Leadership Paradox,* p. 200.

28.  Watts, *Tao: The Watercourse Way,* p. 21.

29.  D. C. Lortie, *Schoolteacher* (Chicago: University of Chicago Press, 1975).

30.  Louis and Miles, *Improving the Urban High School,* 1990.

31.  See Fullan, *The New Meaning of Educational Change,* and Barth, *Improving Schools from Within.*

32.  Morris, Crowson, Porter-Gehrie, and Hurwitz, *Principals in Action.*

33.  Thanks to the summer 1993 organizational theory class at the University of Wisconsin–Madison, Department of Educational Administration, which helped expand on and validate some of these blended roles, and to the principals who spoke to us of their work.

### Chapter Four: Harmonizing the Calendar

1.  Fran Washington is a composite.

2.  This case is a composite of observations of and discussions with hundreds of principals. We have drawn on the common features of principals' work and the ways they blend technical and symbolic roles. We have tried to avoid any examples that are out of the ordinary in order to show how the regular work provides opportunities for extraordinary leadership.

3.  This interesting point is made in Martin Burlingame, "Some Neglected Dimensions in the Study of Educational Administration," *Educational Administration Quarterly,* 1970, *15,* 1–18.

### Chapter Five: The Balanced School

1.  The picture of the school as factory is found in the historical study by Callahan, *Education and the Cult of Efficiency,* whereas the value basis is shown in Beck and Murphy, *Understanding the Principalship,* and William W. Cutler, "Cathedral of Culture: The School House in American Educational Thought and Practice Since 1820," *History of Educational Quarterly,* 1989, *29,* 1–40.

2.   See Wise, *Legislated Learning,* for some of the problems associated with this technical emphasis.

3.   The importance of maintaining this level of external support is noted in J. Meyer and B. Rowan's work, "Institutionalized Organization: Formal Structure as Myth and Ceremony," *American Journal of Sociology, 83,* 340–363.

4.   See the classic studies by Lortie (*Schoolteacher*) and J. W. Little, "Norms of Collegiality and Experimentation: Workplace Conditions of School Success," *American Educational Research Journal, 19*(3), 325–340, for a more lengthy discussion of the norms of collegiality, performance, improvement, and individualism. The norms of inertia and mediocrity are ones that we described as opposites of the others.

5.   Kent D. Peterson and Judith L. Martin, "Institutionalization of Change in Everyday Schools," paper presented at the annual University Council for Educational Administration convention, Minneapolis, 1992.

6.   Terrence E. Deal and Kent D. Peterson, "Technical and Symbolic Aspects of School Improvement," occasional paper, National Center for Effective Schools, Wisconsin Center for Education Research, University of Wisconsin–Madison, 1993.

7.   See Louis and Miles, *Improving the Urban High School.*

8.   The study by Anne Trask, "Principals, Teachers, and Supervision: Dilemmas and Solutions," *The Administrator's Notebook,* 1964, *13,* 1–4, was one of the first to note this function of supervision.

9.   Data from research being conducted at the Center on Organization and Restructuring of Schools, Wisconsin Center for Education Research, University of Wisconsin–Madison.

10.   Deal and Peterson, *The Principal's Role in Shaping Culture.*

11.   Kent D. Peterson and Judith Martin, "Institutionalization of Change in Everyday Schools," unpublished manuscript, University of Wisconsin–Madison.

12.   Data from research being conducted at the Center on Organization and Restructuring of Schools, Wisconsin Center for Education Research, University of Wisconsin–Madison.

13.   See Little, "Norms of Collegiality."

14.  The story of Boyden is well detailed in John McPhee, *The Headmaster* (New York: Farrar, Straus & Giroux, 1966).
15.  Data from research being conducted at the Center on Organization and Restructuring of Schools, Wisconsin Center for Education Research, University of Wisconsin–Madison.
16.  Deal and Peterson, *The Principal's Role in Shaping Culture.*
17.  This memorandum was shared with the authors and is reprinted with permission.
18.  For a stimulating historical discussion of play in culture, see Johan Huizenga, *Homo Ludens: A Study of the Play Element in Culture* (Boston: Beacon Press, 1955).

## Chapter Six: Getting There

1.  Terrence E. Deal and Samuel C. Nutt, *Promoting, Guiding and Surviving Change in School Districts* (Cambridge, Mass.: Abt Associates, 1979).
2.  Niccolò Machiavelli, *The Prince* (London: Penguin Books, 1983), p. 51.
3.  The number of studies and books on organizational change, improvement, and the role of leadership in those efforts runs in the hundreds. They have expanded our understanding of the challenges facing leaders during improvement efforts. See Kenneth A. Leithwood and Deborah J. Montgomery, "The Role of the Elementary School Principal in Program Improvement," *Review of Educational Research,* 1982, *52,* 309–339; Fullan, *The New Meaning of Educational Change*; and Louis and Miles, *Improving the Urban High School.* See Corbett, Dawson, and Firestone, *School Context and School Change,* for some of the challenges faced in improvement efforts. In their study of school context, *Change and Effectiveness in Schools,* Rossman, Corbett, and Firestone also note important roles and tasks that face principals in the midst of change efforts. Also see Matthew B. Miles, "Forty Years of Change in Schools: Some Personal Reflections," *Educational Administration Quarterly,* 1993, *29*(2), 213–248.
4.  Fullan, *The New Meaning of Educational Change.*
5.  Fullan, *The New Meaning of Educational Change.*

6. Corbett, Dawson, and Firestone, *School Context and School Change.*

7. Peterson and Martin, 1992.

8. Fullan, *The New Meaning of Educational Change.*

9. Deal and Peterson, *The Principal's Role in Shaping Culture.*

# Index